MINISTRY OF AGRICULTURE, FISHERIES

Badgers, cattle and tuberculosis

Report to
The Right Honourable Peter Walker, MBE, MP

by Lord Zuckerman O.M.
MA, MD, DSc, FRCP, FRS

President

The Zoological Society of London
and
The Fauna Preservation Society

August 1980

London: Her Majesty's Stationery Office

ISBN 0 11 240355 7

Contents

Preface

The Rt. Hon Peter Walker MP
Minister of Agriculture, Fisheries and Food 26 August 1980

Dear Minister,

In your Press Notice of 25 September 1979, you referred to your concern about criticisms of your Department's policy "for dealing with badgers infected with bovine tuberculosis", criticism which focused "on the extent to which infected badgers are likely to pass on the disease to cattle and on the methods used to eradicate the disease". You went on to say that you had therefore asked me, as President of the Zoological Society of London, "to take an objective look at the problem" and to give you my advice about "the way it should be tackled in the future. I propose", you said, "to make his findings public".

In presenting my report, I should like to record my thanks to your officials for their forbearance and patience in meeting my insistent requests for more and more information. I should also like to express my gratitude to Mr Brian Harding for seeing that my various demands were met, for his help in arranging the many visits and meetings which were necessary in the course of my enquiry, for keeping a record of all that passed, and for checking all the facts that I have received.

ZUCKERMAN

1 Background

1. The suppression of tuberculosis (TB) in cattle is one of many factors that have played a part in reducing the prevalence of the disease in man. Thirty years ago, the number of new human cases that were notified annually in the United Kingdom was about 50,000. Today it is closer to 10,000. But in spite of the decline in its incidence and of the introduction of new methods of therapy, tuberculosis is still a serious affliction. World-wide it remains one of the most persistent of all the scourges of mankind. In India it is said to be responsible for more than half a million deaths a year.

2. While most cases of tuberculosis in man are due to one particular strain of the tubercle bacillus, it had been recognised well before the turn of the century that the disease can also be readily transmitted to human beings, and especially to infants, through the drinking of milk contaminated with the bovine strain of the organism. The UK was slower than some other countries in tackling this particular source of infection which, during the thirties, is estimated to have accounted every year for some 2,500 deaths and at least 4,000 new human TB cases. Germany, Denmark, Sweden and the United States had taken action before we did.

3. Quite apart from the misery it causes, caring for TB patients implied, and still implies – even if to a lesser extent – a high cost in manpower and in physical resources. There is also the loss to the farming community and to the national economy that results from the mandatory slaughter of cattle which veterinary tests show to be infected. The first Government Order to control the disease in cattle was made in 1913, but it had to be revoked in the following year when war erupted. Some four years after the end of hostilities, a new Order, the so-called Milk Order, was made in 1923 with the object of encouraging the voluntary eradication of TB in dairy herds. It allowed for the sale at a premium of milk that had been derived solely from animals that had passed the newly-introduced tuberculin test. Two years later, a further Order demanded the compulsory notification and subsequent slaughter of all dairy cattle exhibiting manifest signs of the disease.

4. Unfortunately, this first phase of the battle to eradicate bovine TB was only moderately successful, for the good and simple reason that large numbers of cattle were spreading the disease without ever exhibiting external signs of tuberculous infection. In 1932, a Committee on Cattle Diseases was accordingly set up under the chairmanship of the President of the Royal Society, Professor Sir Frederick Gowland Hopkins, a Nobel Laureate and one of the most distinguished biochemists of this century.

1

5. The Committee's task was to consider measures which could reduce the incidence of diseases that were responsible for shortening the milking life of a dairy cow to only half of what it might have been under ideal conditions. Particular attention was paid to bovine tuberculosis, about which the Committee decided that only its total eradication from all herds would solve the problem of milk contaminated with the tubercle bacillus. A year later the Medical Research Council (the MRC) issued a report which declared that a pure and wholesome milk supply was a major aim of preventive medicine. According to the Council, there was no single approach to this goal other than deriving our milk supply solely from healthy cows managed under the best sanitary conditions. "The ideal to be aimed at", so the MRC said, "is the removal not only of every obvious source, but also of every discoverable or potential source of infection in the herd." Pasteurisation was then regarded as only a second, even if indispensible, line of defence. The study of tuberculosis in cattle and other farm livestock then became a high research priority for the Agricultural Research Council (the ARC), which had been established in 1931. A Joint ARC/MRC Committee on Tuberculosis was immediately appointed in place of the former MRC Committee.

6. The tuberculin test had been developed before the 1933 MRC Report appeared. It provided a means of diagnosing the existence of tuberculous infection in cattle before they exhibited external or other obvious signs of the disease. The test was also applicable to human beings. Beginning in 1929, the Council had accordingly sponsored a three-year experiment in Ayrshire, in an area of nine square miles which contained 37 dairy farms. All cattle in the 30 farms which co-operated in the investigation were tuberculin tested at six-monthly intervals, and those that showed a positive reaction were culled and then autopsied. The experiment proved that herds could be rid of the disease at a cost to the owners that was more than offset by the greater value of the clean stock that remained. In 1935, it was accordingly decided to embark on a national, but voluntary, programme of attesting herds as being free of tuberculosis. This second phase of the attack on bovine TB had barely been launched before it had to be halted on the outbreak of war in 1939. By then, some 5,000 herds in the country had been attested as free of tuberculosis, with a bonus allowed for the milk they produced.

7. The effort to increase the number of attested herds on a voluntary basis was resumed when the war ended in 1945. In 1950, the Government decided to launch a compulsory campaign of so-called 'area eradication', to be implemented by the Animal Health Division of the Ministry of Agriculture and Fisheries. Areas were to be declared 'attested' after all animals which gave a positive reaction to the tuberculin test had been removed for slaughter, and as soon as two successive tests of each animal had shown that all herds were clean. The scheme succeeded so well that by 1 October 1960 the whole of the United Kingdom was declared 'attested'. This did not mean that the disease had disappeared. What it meant was that the incidence of reactors had declined to what was regarded as negligible proportions. Thus, in 1961, only some 15,000 out of 9,230,000 cattle which were tested throughout the country reacted positively and had to be slaughtered (Appendix I, Table 1). In other words, the overall prevalence of tuberculosis in

dairy herds had by then fallen to less than a fifth of a per cent, as compared with an estimate of 40 per cent at the time of the Gowland Hopkins enquiry of 1932. As a direct consequence of this dramatic decline, and to a lesser extent of the parallel improvement in the control of such other diseases as brucellosis, the dairy industry has been able to expand and its productivity to increase. Compared with the 1950s, we now have some 30 per cent more cattle, and the average milk yield per cow has increased by some 70 per cent. Today there are more than 1,000 units in Great Britain with more than 500 cattle in each, an expansion which could never have been contemplated unless tuberculosis was being effectively controlled.

8. In those parts of the country where herds remained clean, tuberculin testing was continued annually, and in some areas then reduced to two-yearly and even three-yearly intervals. But the improvement was not uniform. Indeed, in 1961, the year after the whole of the country had been declared a single attested area, the incidence of reactors in the South West of England was far higher than the national average, and four times higher in the case of Cornwall (Appendix I, Table 1). In 1970, a special and intensive field-study by MAFF veterinarians was therefore organised to enquire into this unsatisfactory situation. The West Penwith Peninsula of Cornwall, where both the density of livestock and the incidence of reactors were exceptionally high, was selected as the area where an effort would be made to uncover the causes of the continuing 'breakdowns' — the term used by MAFF to denote an outbreak of TB in a herd. The team reported in 1972, but their enquiry proved to be of little practical value. It was found that young cattle were the most susceptible to infection; that fences were generally in a poor state, making contact between animals of neighbouring farms all too easy; and that standards of husbandry and management were in general poor. One of the team's main recommendations was that tuberculin tests should be made every three months in order to detect the disease before it had time to spread. The team also recommended that even 'doubtful reactors' should be removed for slaughter. Another recommendation was that the examination of wild life, especially badgers and rats, as well as livestock should continue in areas of high-reactor density to see whether any species constituted a reservoir of the bovine tubercle bacillus.

9. It so happened that just as the team was completing its work, an observant Gloucestershire farmer, frustrated at repeated failures to trace the source of breakdowns in his cattle, and concerned about his consequential financial losses, had got the idea that badgers with setts on his land might be a source of infection. In 1971 he took one that had died in the open to the MAFF Animal Health Office in Gloucester, where a post-mortem examination revealed that the animal was riddled with tuberculous lesions. Cultures made at MAFF's Central Veterinary Laboratory showed that the particular bacillus by which the animal had been infected was the same strain of tubercle bacillus *(Mycobacterium bovis)* as is found in cattle. Soon more tuberculous badgers were found, and in the spring of 1972 a systematic survey was carried out to determine the extent to which Gloucestershire badgers were affected. In one particular area, one in three of the creatures was found to have the disease, while in the rest of Gloucestershire the infection rate was one in six. Cultures were also made from badger droppings,

3

and a variety of other wild mammals were collected for laboratory examination, with tuberculous lesions being found in a few specimens. Badger carcases collected in other parts of the country were also examined, but in general it was only in the South West, where the badger population is particularly dense (Appendix II), that significant numbers of tuberculous specimens were recovered. In one case, every member of a social group, including young, was found to be infected. (Appendix I, Tables 3, 5, 9.)

10. While all these enquiries were going on, a series of important complementary experimental studies was started. These showed that healthy badgers can be made tuberculous by inoculating them intravenously with a culture of the tubercle bacillus isolated from cattle; that healthy badgers can contract the disease when housed with experimentally infected badgers; and that calves penned with experimentally or naturally infected tuberculous badgers will contract the disease.

11. Tuberculosis strikes different animals in different ways. In the badger, the disease usually spreads rapidly, with the lungs and kidneys (and their associated lymph glands) being particularly vulnerable to the bovine strain of the bacillus. As a result, it takes a form that can be likened to the human condition commonly known as 'galloping consumption'. Enough is known about the epidemiology of tuberculosis in general to realise how the disease can spread from one badger to another when infection has occurred. Once an animal is infected it will communicate the disease to others which live in the same sett, either by exhaling the organism in its breath, or by discharging it in its saliva, in bronchial pus, in urine and in faeces. The organism can also survive outside the body, and MAFF scientists have succeeded in isolating the bacillus from samples of badger bedding, faeces and from four- to six-week old carcases. In 1976 it was also found that cultures of the bovine tubercle bacillus can be grown from the grass of permanent pasture experimentally contaminated with badger urine. These cultures were successful only with grass pulled up by the roots during the winter months; in the summer the organism does not seem to remain viable on grass for more than a few days. It is also well known that animals from one social group which stray into another often get into fights – particularly adult males – and wounds infected with the bacillus have also been found to be fairly common. That is one way the disease spreads between neighbouring social groups.

12. Every bit as striking as all these findings were the correlations that emerged from field studies of the geographical relationships of herds in which breakdown had occurred to setts containing badgers that turned out to be tuberculous. Thus, in 160 breakdowns in Avon and Gloucestershire during 1976, infected badgers were found within a radius of 0.75 km of affected herds in 113 cases (and within 1.5 km in a further 15 cases). Another common observation is that herds which had been subject to breakdown over many years become clean and healthy when all the badgers which previously had roamed their pastures have been removed. A collateral observation is that in counties other than those of the South West there is a high correlation between breakdowns of unknown origin and the density of setts in the vicinity of the affected herds — an observation which suggests that badger TB may be more widespread than is commonly supposed.

13. In Appendix III, I have set out further information about these correlations, and have reproduced some letters that have been sent to me by farmers. The Tables set out in Appendix I also apply.

14. The evidence underlying the policy to get rid of badgers where they appear to have been responsible for breakdowns has been published in several scientific and other journals. During the course of my enquiry much additional information which I wanted has been provided by members of MAFF's veterinary staff. The publications to which I have referred are listed in Appendix X.

2 The Ministry's Responsibilities

15. The authority of the Ministry to take such steps as it deems necessary in tracing the source of infection when a tuberculous breakdown occurs in a herd derives from the Diseases of Animals Act 1950. The drill is that not before all other possible sources have been eliminated, and only when infected badger setts are found within a given radius of the farm concerned, are consultations begun which could lead to a decision to kill badgers. The procedures that are followed are set out in Appendix IV. The legal basis for the badger control measures rests in Section 9 of the Badgers Act 1973, as amended by Section 16 of the Conservation of Wild Animals and Wild Plants Act 1975. In effect, the Minister is empowered to issue licences for the killing of badgers by means of poison gas for the purpose of preventing the spread of disease. The legislation governing these control operations was further augmented by the inclusion of sections in the Agriculture (Miscellaneous Provisions) Act 1976, giving the Minister power of direct entry onto land, in areas defined by Orders made after consulting the Nature Conservancy Council, for the purpose of investigating and killing wild life to prevent the spread of disease. The Badgers (Control Areas) Order 1977 was made under this provision, and established four 'control areas' in the South West in which control operations have been carried out in accordance with the 1976 Act.

16. As a result of an undertaking given by the Government during the passage through Parliament of the Conservation of Wild Animals and Wild Plants Act 1975, the Minister of Agriculture in 1975 set up a Consultative Panel on Badgers and Tuberculosis to provide an independent forum for informed discussion and advice. The organisations represented on the Panel are listed in Appendix V. In addition, the late Earl of Cranbrook, a conservationist, together with two naturalists known for their work on badgers and, later, a microbiologist from one of the London hospitals, were also appointed.

17. It is worth recording that in 1975 a formal complaint against the Ministry for not acting swiftly enough to rid his land of TB-infected badgers was laid by a Dorset farmer before the Parliamentary Commissioner for Administration – the 'Ombudsman' – who ruled that while there had been no unreasonable delay in the investigation of the badgers on the farm, and in spite of being inhibited at the time for lack of parliamentary authority, the Ministry had nonetheless been slow to act once the results of the investigation were known.

3 The Status of the Badger

18. Badgers are among the more striking survivors of the original wild mammalian fauna of Great Britain. The animal enjoyed some protection in England and Wales under the Protection of Animals Act 1911 as amended: (in Scotland under an Act of 1912), which was designed generally to prevent cruelty to animals. The Act prohibited the use of poison to kill mammals, but provided a defence in a court of law for the use of poison to get rid of rats, mice and other small ground vermin. Specific protection for the badger was accorded through an Act of 1973 which, among other things, made the so-called sport of badger-digging and the use of badger tongs, illegal. In the course of the debate on the Private Members Bill that resulted in this Act, it was said that the badger was becoming less numerous in some parts of the country.

19. A few badger-protection societies had started to organise during the period in which the 1973 legislation was making its way to the Statute Book. Their concern was to see that an end was put to badger-baiting and digging; and so to the associated cruelty. No one then regarded these as activities which could lead to the extinction of the species in the United Kingdom. The badger-control legislation of 1975, which empowered the Minister to issue licences for the killing of badgers, was, however, regarded by some as a new threat to an animal about whose welfare many felt deeply. In consequence, several new badger-protection societies were organised, and for the first time one began to hear talk of the extinction of the animal.

20. There is no need for me to describe the protests which were made when officials of your Department tried to gas a sett on common-land, and which led to your asking me to make the enquiry of which this is my report.

21. Following your announcement, the organisations and individuals listed in Appendix IX responded to the Ministry's invitation that written evidence could be sent to me. Much of what I received indicated only too plainly how strongly opposed some people are to the Ministry's policies. The most extreme condemnation came either from self-appointed protection groups or from individuals associated with them. More reasoned, but at the same time critical submissions were sent by the Society for the Promotion of Nature Conservation and by some of its associated County Naturalist Trusts, who between them own or manage over 1,000 Nature Reserves covering nearly 100,000 acres. On the other hand, there were others, including several farmers, who had no doubt that the Ministry was pursuing the right policies. Some felt that action was not sufficiently urgent. In acknowledging the more substantive submissions sent to me, I invited their authors to supplement their written statements by word of mouth if they so wished. As a result, I arranged to meet various groups and individuals, both in London and in different places during the course of visits to the West Country.

4 Do Badgers get TB?

22. Among the doubts and more pertinent assertions and questions that have been raised in opposition to the Ministry's policy are the following:

(a) Badgers do not get TB.

(b) The Ministry's observations to the effect that they do were not controlled.

(c) Badgers do not transmit TB to cattle.

(d) No explanation has been given of instances – called 'anomalies' – when herd breakdowns have occurred in the absence of tuberculous badgers and, conversely, of the finding of tuberculous badgers unassociated with herd breakdowns.

23. I propose to consider the matter of TB in badgers first, and to do so in the form of a question, since some of the individuals and organisations who wrote to me, and with a few of whom I afterwards conferred, fervently believe that the view that the animals can contract the disease is a myth. The strength with which this belief was expressed was matched only by what was clearly a genuine concern for the well-being of badgers and an abhorrence of any form of cruelty. As illustration, I quote from a written submission sent to me by the Cotswold Wildlife Preservation Society – whose representatives I later met – to the effect that "action against the badger" is not only "undertaken without conclusive evidence and proper preliminary research", but is also "unnecessary". Mrs McDonald, a farm-owner on Dartmoor, wrote that she was "far from convinced that the Ministry of Agriculture has succeeded in making out a case against the badger". Again, Lady Sayer, a prominent campaigner for the conservation of Dartmoor, wrote:

> "I can only say that the Ministry of Agriculture's statements condemning the badger for spreading tuberculosis (or brucellosis or foot and mouth or whatever) do not ring true to me. They have not been, and cannot be, proved; they are a 'fail-safe' hit-and-miss excuse for carrying out a policy determined by officials working in the dark, but resolved on badger extermination as a means – whether mistaken or not – of eliminating one 'possible' source of infection among very many. It is all guesswork and it causes cruelty and suffering."

24. On practically every occasion that it was made, the rejection of MAFF's findings that the bovine tubercle bacillus can infect badgers seemed to have been based on widely-quoted statements made by a Mrs. Ruth Murray to the effect that over a period of twenty-two years she had never encountered the disease in a badger. In these statements reference was usually made to more than 200 post-mortems of badgers that Mrs. Murray had carried out. In the 1973 debate in which he introduced his Badger Protection Bill, Lord Arran referred to Mrs.

8

Murray as one of the greatest badger experts in Britain. Two years after the passage of the Bill, Mrs. Murray unsuccessfully brought an action against the Minister of Agriculture and one of his officials for alleged cruelty to the animal.

25. When my review was announced, Mrs. Murray did not respond to the invitation to provide written evidence, but on learning of her interest, I got in touch with her and she kindly agreed to a meeting in order to discuss her findings. This took place at her home on Dartmoor, where we were joined by Dr. Plowright, a member of the research staff of the Agricultural Research Council, who has worked extensively on virus diseases and their transmission from wild animals in Africa to domesticated livestock — for example, cattle plague, African swine fever, and malignant catarrhal fever.

26. Three hours of talk, in which Mrs. Murray was joined by her husband, a retired farmer, unfortunately elicited no facts. I explained that I had heard that she had never encountered TB in a badger (she admitted that she did not have the requisite training to recognise a TB lesion, implying that she relied for her views on veterinary advice). I told her that in the course of a post-mortem of a badger I had had demonstrated to me obvious TB, and that I had examined microscopic specimens of typical lesions. I also informed her that since the first case, about which she had expressed doubts, several hundred post-mortems had been carried out on badgers with TB, and that much had been published in reputable scientific journals. None of this encouraged Mrs. Murray to change her stance; she seemed to imply that if tuberculous badgers had been autopsied, the creatures might have been artificially infected, as if some gigantic hoax had been perpetrated by the Ministry's veterinary officers and scientists in their efforts to establish the badger as the 'culprit' responsible for breakdowns in herds of cattle. If I had seen tuberculous lesions in a badger, I was, by implication, now included among those who were party to the hoax. Mrs. Murray declined repeated requests which I made verbally to allow me to read her 200 records of post-mortems, the majority of which I understood to have been of animals killed on the roads. She also failed to acknowledge letters I sent after the visit, one immediately after, and the third by recorded delivery, in which I repeated my request. She also refused to allow me to see the badgers she is said to keep on her premises, contenting herself by bringing into the room one tame animal only. I was subsequently told that she had refused invitations to inspect tuberculous badger carcases at MAFF's Starcross Veterinary Investigation Centre in March 1978 and July 1979, and that she had also declined to meet the Consultative Panel in October 1976 and February 1977 in order to discuss her data. Subsequently I learnt that in the course of cross-examination in the action for cruelty which she brought against the Minister in 1975, she did not deny the proposition that badgers could contract and transmit bovine TB, and that consequently it had not been necessary to call on the Ministry's expert witnesses to provide evidence about the occurrence of the disease in the animal.

27. I have dealt at length with this episode in my enquiry because no other group or individual who shared the view that badgers do not contract TB claimed that their denial was founded on veterinary advice. On what authority Mrs. Murray bases her much-quoted views I do not know. She has declined to give me the

name or names of the veterinarians she has consulted, nor have they come forward.

28. But even if it were the case that Mrs. Murray's representatives had closely examined 200 badgers for tuberculous infection and had found them all free of the disease, it would not alter the fact that other badgers have been autopsied and have been proved to be tuberculous; that cultures have been made from their lesions; that these have been typed and the causative organism proved to be the bovine tubercle bacillus; and that tuberculous badgers can pass the disease to previously-uninfected calves.

29. What I have said about Mrs. Murray adds little to what is reported by the Royal Society for the prevention of Cruelty to Animals (the RSPCA) in its recently published booklet, *Badgers & Bovine Tuberculosis,* which was based upon an enquiry carried out by the organisation's Wild Animals Advisory Committee (WAAC). I quote:

"Apart from Mrs Ruth Murray, all witnesses accepted the veterinary evidence that badgers do suffer from tuberculosis of the bovine strain. Mrs. Murray said that, throughout the period of her studies since 1955, any badger either wild-caught and brought to her, or captive which had either died or been destroyed, had been subjected to a full post-mortem examination by qualified veterinary or laboratory personnel. She said post-mortem investigations are routine procedures with all carcasses brought to her attention yet, at no single time in the 22 years of her intensive studies of the badger, had a single specimen been identified as suffering from tuberculosis. She said her sample was a truly random sample because the badgers came from places far apart in Britain, with the majority of specimens from the southwest region, and she posed the question why she had not encountered one badger infected with tuberculosis.

"Mrs. Murray's evidence might seem to be at variance with that of the Ministry, but the Committee concluded that her experience was not unexpected. In the first place, her sample was not random as the term is normally understood. Further, bovine tuberculosis might not be found in a diseased carcass, even by veterinarians, in a routine post-mortem examination, because specialised techniques are needed to detect the presence of the causal organism. . . It seems that the examination of casually collected corpses is not an effective method for the detection of tuberculosis in badgers.

"Members of WAAC accept that the experimental evidence demonstrates conclusively the susceptibility of badgers to tubercle bacilli of the bovine strain, and are satisfied that naturally occurring infections are found in wild badgers."

30. In the light of this RSPCA Report and of what I myself have learnt, I find it extraordinary that Mrs. Murray's unsubstantiated assertions about badgers and tuberculosis have carried so much weight among the badger-protection societies.

31. Here I must note that not one of more than 40 badgers examined by Dr. McDiarmid, who has recently retired from the Agricultural Research Council's

Institute for Research on Animal Diseases, and which were collected over a period of some 35 years for the specific purpose of searching for tuberculous infection in wild animals, was found to harbour the causative organism. All the animals which he studied came from Oxfordshire, Berkshire and Hampshire. Being a trained scientist, Dr. McDiarmid does not take his negative observations as meaning that badgers in the South Western part of the country do not get TB. Negative findings cannot upturn positive conclusions derived from properly controlled scientific observation and experiment.

5 No Controls?

32. This brings me to another misunderstanding about MAFF's procedures which disturbs some by whom they are condemned. Several of those who made submissions insisted that the laboratory work by which the Government's policy is underpinned was not 'controlled', and that it was only after the idea that badgers could pass the bovine tubercle bacillus to cattle took hold that MAFF sought evidence to back it up.

33. I have no hesitation in saying that the work was properly 'controlled', using the term as it applies in scientific discourse. So far as I can make out, the sense in which the word 'control' has been used by those who protest MAFF's policy is that of supervision or oversight by an independent body – in some submissions, the implication is that the protesters themselves should be the 'controllers'. Such a suggestion would seem strange to a working scientist, or to anyone familiar with the scientific process. Published reports of the work that was done by Government scientists are there to be read by anyone experienced in epidemiological studies, and competent to understand pathological and bacteriological procedures. If any scientist had doubts about what was reported, there was nothing to stop him from arranging his own post-mortem studies. I cannot imagine that MAFF scientists and veterinarians would fail to help in such an arrangement, or that they would deny any scientist access to their records, preparations, or other material; or correspondingly, that other scientists and veterinarians would refuse the Ministry access to the results of their studies.

34. Mrs. Murray's refusals were the only ones I encountered in the course of my enquiry.

35. The second part of the criticism – that MAFF veterinarians arbitrarily decided that badgers were in some way involved and then sought evidence to back up the idea – also reveals a lack of understanding of the scientific process. Whatever the branch of science in which he works, the researcher is always trying to shed light on what may be obscure. He will hit upon an idea, however vague or however precise, stimulated by something that he may have read, or by something which he may have observed, or by something that he may have been told by another scientist. He then sets the idea out as a working hypothesis, which he will try to validate or disprove, either by experiment or by further observation, or by correlation techniques. This he does in order to see whether he is on the right track (i.e. whether he can validate his hypothesis), or whether his hunch needs to be discarded. In the present instance, the badger that was autopsied in 1971 turned out to have lesions which looked tuberculous. The staining of microscopic sections by methods appropriate for the tubercle bacillus showed that the lesions were indeed caused by an organism with the appearance of a tubercle bacillus. If the result had been otherwise, the men in the laboratory

would have searched in a different direction. But in the following step the bacillus turned out to be the bovine strain. Had it proved to be avian, or even human, the next experimental step in the enquiry would have taken a course different from the one it did. Further autopsies then showed that the 1971 badger was not unique, but that TB is common in badgers in parts of the South West.

36. If this is the process which those who protest against MAFF's policy now condemn, then I can only say that MAFF scientists are to be commended for having set about their work in the way of all good and experienced scientists.

6 Do Badgers transmit TB to Cattle?

37. From the evidence that has been put before me, I am satisfied that badgers can contract TB and transmit it both among themselves and to cattle. Some who are prepared to accept this proposition, but who are opposed to MAFF's policies, ask, however, whether the animals do so under field conditions. In theory it is possible to conceive of an experiment which, even though it would be very costly, should give a final answer to this question. But I fear that however it turned out, there might still be some who by nature are not able to accept what in science is called 'objective truth'. In spite of the photographs taken of our globe from outer space, in spite of the testimony of those who have walked on the moon, there are probably people who, believing that the world is flat, claim that the pictures were faked, and the moon-walking a hoax.

38. But having now critically considered all the evidence, and having cross-examined many who are concerned, the only conclusion that I myself can draw is that badgers do transmit the disease in the field. I do so for the following reasons, and I believe that the evidence is adequate.

Argument by Exclusion

39. Before wildlife was suspected as being a reservoir of the disease, efforts to find the source of infection in a particular herd breakdown, or the reasons for the frequency of breakdowns in the South West, often ended in failure. They still do, even in areas where the population of badgers is very high, and where badger setts and ranges of movement of badgers intrude on pasture land and even farm buildings (see Appendix I, Table 10).

40. Herd breakdowns have become relatively rare events, and massive breakdowns even rarer (see Appendix I, Table 2). They are nonetheless dangerous because of the possibility of spread – even without any relaxation of present control measures – and they can be very costly to the farmer. Wherever and whenever they occur, it is, as I have said, the duty of the Minister's officials to seek any probable or possible cause. This is done with the help of a check-list of some 20 possibilities, all of which are based on past experience (Appendix IV).

41. The search begins with a survey of the history of the herd to discover whether it has suffered previous breakdowns, with an enquiry into the histories of the herds from which reactors originated, and into the histories of other herds in the locality concerned. The records of new purchases are examined, as is the nature of summer grazings and the possibility of straying. Other possibilities that are considered are the spread of infection from sewage plants and cesspits, from slaughterhouse wastes, or from animals such as rats, cats and dogs – and even

from human beings. Five cases where the origin of bovine TB infection in cattle was traced to an infected farm-worker were recorded between 1972 and 1978. Enquiries into these and other likely causes are made before attention is paid to the possibility that wildlife may be implicated. Now that the badger is known to be susceptible to the disease (I shall deal later with the question of creatures other than badgers), a search is made for setts either on the farm itself or on contiguous land from which the creatures might roam onto the pastures grazed by the herd which has suffered a breakdown. If any setts are discovered, and are found to be inhabited, a few badgers are caught by MAFF officers. The animals are then killed and autopsied. If bovine TB is diagnosed, the local Water and other Authorities are notified before cyanide gassing is started. I am told that these preliminary enquiries may take as long as six months. The procedures followed in gassing and regassing are laid out formally, and need not be detailed here.

42. The enquiry into a breakdown is called off if a likely source is identified before the stage is reached of considering the possibility that badgers are responsible for the outbreak. This means that if the source of the trouble is diagnosed either as a 'bought-in' beast or as one that was introduced as a calf from a clean herd which had previously suffered a breakdown, there still remains a chance that badgers which forage on a farm might also be tuberculous. They would remain unidentified. Another point that has struck me is that a delay of up to six months before known infected setts are dealt with provides an opportunity for the spread of the disease both among badgers and cattle, although the latter will be subjected to regular tuberculin tests.

The Evidence of Association

43. I am informed that between January 1976, the first full year of gassing operations, and December 1979, 185 out of 2,432 badgers that had been collected in the vicinity of 477 farms where breakdowns had occurred revealed tuberculous lesions at autopsy. In those cases where typing was carried out, the causative organism was always the bovine tubercle bacillus. This consitutes one aspect of the association of bovine TB in badgers and cattle.

44. Another is the fact that the incidence of breakdowns in affected farms has declined dramatically after the clearance of setts which prior sampling had shown had been the home of infected badgers. A few specific and well-publicised exercises of this kind are widely quoted. In addition, I have been shown the records of several smaller clearance operations where breakdowns have ceased to occur in dairy herds after the removal of badgers (Appendix III; also Appendix I, Tables 4, 6, 7 and 8).

The Chain of Evidence

45. Some of what I have called 'evidence of association' is anecdotal in nature. I have therefore asked several medical and veterinary colleagues with experience of diseases which are transmitted by animals, such as, for example, malaria, bilharzia and rinderpest, whether the chain of evidence which implicates the

badger as a reservoir of bovine TB in the affected counties of the South West is capable of any other interpretation. For the following reasons the answer has been a uniform 'no'.

(a) The infecting organism has been experimentally proved to be the same in both species – cultures made from TB lesions in cattle have infected badgers experimentally, and *vice versa;*

(b) Badgers develop 'open' lesions and can spread the organism;

(c) They can pass the disease on when placed in contact with clean cattle;

(d) In areas in which infected badgers are common, the infection rate in cattle is high;

(e) If infected badger colonies are removed, the incidence of breakdowns in cattle decreases;

(f) The organism can persist in pasture long enough to allow of infection in cattle.

46. This series of related propositions, in line with what are traditionally known in bacteriological circles as 'Koch's postulates', is no more than is ever demanded in defining the causative sequence of events that may be involved in the transmission of disease from wild animals to man. Such diseases belong to a class often called 'zoonoses', of which glanders is one example, with both horse and man suffering from the same type of severe pulmonary infection. Another is the parasitic infection in humans called schistosomiasis, which may be spread by baboons infected with the parasite *Schistosoma mansoni* and which contaminate streams and ponds with their faeces. Snails then become infected and liberate the next stage of the life cycle of the parasite (cercariae) into the water. People who bathe in the water then pick up the parasite — and the disease.

47. An even more significant and much more striking parallel to what is happening in the counties of the South West is the story that has been uncovered over the past ten years about the transmission of bovine TB in New Zealand. It concerns the opossum, an Australian marsupial that was introduced into New Zealand where it has flourished since the middle of the nineteenth century. This creature has turned out to be a reservoir of the bovine tubercle bacillus.

48. The story begins with the launching by the New Zealand authorities in 1959 of a voluntary scheme to eradicate bovine tuberculosis. The scheme was made compulsory for dairy herds in 1961, and for beef cattle in 1968. At the start of the eradication programme, 11 per cent of all cows tested were found to have the disease. By early 1974 the figure had fallen, overall, to 0.2 per cent.

49. It was soon noticed, however, that the disease persisted in certain isolated areas of the South Island, particularly in the Buller area along the west coast, where, in spite of tuberculin testing at three-monthly intervals, with 'positives' being slaughtered as soon as they were identified, the rate of infection in some herds remained as high as 35 per cent. "This suggested", to quote from one of the documents that has been sent to me, "the presence of an intact active reservoir of infection undisturbed and undisclosed by the testing programme".

50. 'Possums' – as they are called in New Zealand – turned out to be the source of infection. Although it had been known for years that in captivity the animals can catch a virulent form of TB, there was at first no suspicion that they played any part in the transmission of the disease to cattle. A massive TB breakdown in a dairy herd on a farm close to an area where the disease had been found three years earlier in a large percentage of the members of a colony of possums – this was the first time tuberculosis had been discovered in a wild possum – then led to a detailed field and laboratory study of the possible relation of the disease in the possum to that in cattle. It was soon found that once it picks up the tubercle bacillus, a wild possum has little resistance to the spread of the organism to most parts of its body. Dead or moribund possums infected with the disease have been found on pastures grazed by cattle. The lethal organism is always the bovine strain of the tubercle bacillus, and cross-infection from possum to cattle and *vice versa* was soon established in several field experiments in which calves free of the disease were introduced to pasture land where the possum grazed, and across which it moved, and which had either never been grazed by cattle or which had been left ungrazed for some six months. In one such experiment, 29 tuberculin-negative calves that had been left to graze were slaughtered after six months. Gross tuberculous lesions were found in 16. Cross-infection was also later shown to occur by laboratory experiment.

51. A lengthy series of studies, references to which are given in Appendix X, has suggested that cattle first passed the infection to the possum; that the susceptibility of the latter to the bovine tubercle bacillus, combined with high population densities, particularly in 'bush-pasture margins', lead to the rapid spread of the disease in possum colonies; and finally that the disease is passed back to cattle mainly through the contamination of pastures, and sometimes through cattle 'investigating' dead possums that may be lying about. The climate of the west coast of South Island is conducive to the survival of the organism on pasture, and the practice of over-wintering cattle in forests heavily populated by possums increases the likelihood of transmission of the disease from infected animals to cattle. In the latter circumstances, the poor nutritional condition of cattle grazing in the forests, where their diet is not supplemented in any way, increases their susceptibility to infection. It has been suggested that mosquitoes which bite both possums and cattle are also possible vectors of the disease.

52. Each colony of possums normally has a restricted home range, so that outbreaks of possum/cattle TB are usually localised and independent of each other. Until the relationship of the disease in the two mammals was recognised, farmers and trappers may also have spread the disease by collecting possums for their skins, and so moving infected specimens around.

53. With the exception of the hare and the bat, TB has on occasion been found in all species of wild animal in New Zealand. In some, such as wild sheep, the disease was once very common. But today there is no doubt that only possums constitute an important secondary reservoir of TB. What also seems clear is that TB started to infect wild possums only recently, and that the disease in this creature has since become a plague. The task of the New Zealand Government now is to see that cattle which react to the tuberculin test are slaughtered, at the same time as the

affected areas are rid of the possum. This policy is clearly working. Although the campaign has been in progress for less than ten years, the incidence of the disease in dairy and beef herds in the affected areas has already declined significantly. On the other hand, the disease has become so rampant among possums that this has become a problem on its own. No one, of course, has actually seen possums in the actual process of passing tubercle bacilli to a cow, any more than the transfer has been watched in the case of the badger. But the fact that this does happen is nonetheless incontrovertible.

54. The New Zealand authorities were quick to note that the susceptibility of possums to bovine TB was similar to what was being reported about the badger of the South West of England. And it could justifiably be said that the very large part which farming plays in the economy of New Zealand encouraged a more vigorous enquiry into the place of the possum in the epidemiology of the disease than has been carried out so far in the case of the badger. The New Zealand authorities have not had to contend with a lobby organised to contest what is being done.

55. From the start of my enquiry, I have asked myself whether the first badger in which TB was recognised in 1971 was actually the first, or among the first, to be infected. It is a question about which only speculation is possible, although it seems to be the case that some farmers in Cornwall had long suspected that the creature was a carrier of the disease, and that this was the explanation for the herd breakdowns from which they were suffering.

56. This brings me to questions that have been put to me several times. How is it that badgers suffering from TB have been found in other parts of the country unassociated with herd breakdowns? Why is it that MAFF treats the badger as a 'scapegoat' only in the South West? In repeated criticisms of Government policy, the Western Daily Press, which has long concerned itself with the problem, has also suggested that the MAFF was not only slow in investigating the 'badger connection' which farmers had long suspected, but also confused and haphazard in the manner of its enquiries.

57. This last criticism was made to me with the clear qualification that it comes from a lay quarter. But nonetheless it needs answering. Were MAFF officials lax in not spotting sooner than they did that badgers are a reservoir of TB infection in the South West? Should the team of four veterinarians who were enquiring into the problem in the West Penwith Peninsula of Cornwall before the disease was diagnosed in Gloucestershire be judged incompetent because the bovine tubercle bacillus was not found in the tissues of any one of 69 wild mammals, or in any of 24 different badger droppings which they collected? I think not – any more than I am prepared to regard myself as negligent because I do not propose to follow up some of the folk-lore that I have picked up during the course of my enquiry – for example, that badgers gnaw at the udders of ewes. The MAFF team had properly discussed the problem of herd breakdowns not only with local branches of the National Farmers' Union, with the local authorities, and with other professional staff of the Ministry, but also with a number of livestock owners as well as veterinary surgeons in private practice. Whatever some Cornish farmers may

have believed about the animal there is no indication that any of the people who were consulted suspected that badgers harboured the bovine tubercle bacillus. As it so happened, the lead which directed the attention of the team to wildlife as a reservoir of infection came from the report of a positive finding in Gloucestershire. From that moment, the team of four veterinarians acted. It is to be regretted that none of the specimens which they examined (including two badgers) revealed the presence of the tubercle bacillus, but their report does make the recommendation that wildlife should be studied more extensively than they had had the opportunity of doing. And that is what has since been done, even if the search could have been pursued more vigorously than it has been.

58. It is easy to make retrospective criticisms about the way scientific knowledge is gained, and about the priorities of scientific enquiry. Only too often is it imagined that what is known now should always have been obvious. The truth is the exact opposite. The road to valid scientific understanding is very rarely direct. The anopheles mosquito was experienced only as a troublesome stinging insect before it was discovered that it was the vector for the organism that is responsible for malaria. Monkeys were regarded as amusing, if at times troublesome and vicious pets, before it was found that some of them harbour dangerous viral diseases, such as yellow fever, or the more recently discovered B virus which causes fatal encephalitis in man, or the Marburg virus, named after the tragic spate of deaths in laboratory workers in the city of that name. Koch, the German bacteriologist who in 1882 discovered the tubercle bacillus, held that the bovine strain could not infect human beings. Other bacteriologists took a contrary view, as did a Royal Commission which reported in 1911. Twenty years later, Blacklock, in a study of 1,800 autopsies of Glasgow children, found that the bovine strain was four times more responsible for abdominal tuberculous lesions than was the human strain.

59. Bovine TB was not diagnosed in the wild badger until a specific search was made for it by an experienced pathologist whose eyes were open to the possibility that tuberculous lesions in the animal need not necessarily have the same appearance as those in cattle. It is very possible that other badgers suffering from TB had been 'opened' by zoologists concerned with, say, the state of the reproductive organs, but that the condition was missed because it was not being looked for. And the same is true of the possum. In science, 'there always has to be a first time'. No one can foretell which other creatures will turn out to be reservoirs of germs of as yet unknown, not to mention already recognised, human diseases.

Population Density

60. Clearly one likely explanation for the close correlation between the occurrence of the disease in badgers and herd breakdowns in the South West is population density. About a quarter of the country's total dairy herd is to be found in the areas concerned. These, by general consent, are also the parts of the country most densely populated by badgers (Appendix II). The argument goes as follows:

(a) Badgers are highly susceptible to the bovine tubercle bacillus, and the resulting infection takes a violent form which encourages the rapid spread of the infective organism.

(b) The animals live in small social groups in one or a small number of associated setts. These provide conditions highly conducive to the infection of all members of a group, once one has contracted the disease. Cubs are particularly vulnerable.

(c) The more densely populated an area by badgers, the more constrained will be the territory or home-range of each social group and the more likely will boundary disputes occur. Infection could be spread from group to group, (1) because fighting may result in tuberculous wounds, (2) because infected animals could move into setts contiguous with those of another group, and (3) because young animals, particularly males, are believed to leave their parental groups fairly early, so helping to spread infection.

(d) Badgers and cattle often share the same habitat. They forage over the same pastures. Earthworms are a preferred item of diet for badgers but, particularly in times of drought, they search for dung-beetles in dry cowpats. They also eat various pasture plants.

(e) Quite apart from grass contaminated by the urine and sputum of infected badgers, demarcation lines between two social groups of the creature are often preferred sites for the latrines they make. These may be in pastures which are grazed by cattle.

(f) On present evidence, badgers are the only wild species which in the South West are known to serve as a reservoir for the bovine tubercle bacillus in cattle.

61. I have set out these six propositions as they have struck me in my survey of the badger problem. They happen to be much the same as those the New Zealand authorities have found to apply to the tuberculous possum. If any one proposition proved significantly different from what it appears to be, the chain in the transmission of the tubercle bacillus from cattle to badgers (or possums), from badger to badger (or possum) and from the wild animal back to cattle might be different.

62. One inference I would draw from the fact that Dr. McDiarmid did not encounter a single case of TB in the badgers which he collected in the course of his lengthy and systematic search for the occurrence of tuberculous infection in wild animals, is that while dairy and beef cattle might well have been infected – even if at a declining rate because of the TB eradication programme – the density of the badger population in the areas from which the animals he autopsied came was significantly less than it is in the parts of the South West which are now the problem, with a significantly lesser probability of any interaction with cattle. It is also possible that farms carrying dairy and beef herds were (as they are today) more dispersed in the counties studied by Dr. McDiarmid than they are in Cornwall, Devon, Gloucestershire, Somerset and Avon. Another possibility is that badgers outside the South West might have been previously infected and achieved a measure of immunity, and that the level of infection fell in parallel with the decline of the disease in cattle. A further possibility is that in recent years

the bovine bacillus has in some way become more adapted for infection of badgers and to spread among badgers.

The Regional Incidence of TB in Badgers

63. At the time of Dr. McDiarmid's enquiry there was no information about the regional prevalence of bovine TB in badgers. There is insufficient now. Such as has been derived from the examination of corpses of badgers killed on the road, and reported by members of the public to MAFF Veterinary Investigation Centres, can hardly be regarded as providing a representative picture of the distribution of the disease in the badgers of the United Kingdom (Appendix I, Table 3). In some counties where badgers are rare, people may not even have heard that MAFF will collect for examination all badger carcases reported on roads or in fields. In others, particularly in the South West, interest in the subject is clearly very strong, and is reflected in the figures for 'recoveries'. Even if it were assumed that the populations of badgers and cattle were evenly distributed over the country, one would also have to take into account the fact that the density of motor traffic varies from county to county, as would consequently the frequency of road deaths.

64. In the ideal, we would all like to have a series of maps of the country with overlays for different years, reaching back to before the start of the campaign to eradicate bovine tuberculosis, showing (1) the distribution of dairy and beef herds, (2) the prevalence of the disease in cattle, (3) the distribution of badger social groups (with an indication of those which were tuberculous), (4) the distribution of herd breakdowns, and (5) their relation to the occurrence of badgers, healthy and unhealthy.

65. Unfortunately, maps of this kind do not exist. We can deal only with the present. Such information as exists about the distribution of badgers has either been collected by the Mammal Society (Appendix II) or can be inferred from the distribution of badger carcases sent in for examination to MAFF's Veterinary Investigation Centres (Appendix I, Table 3). The Mammal Society map is recognised as being deficient in detail. A map of the distribution of setts in Devon shown me by the Devon Trust for Nature Conservation seemed to suggest that it had been constructed by a keen naturalist who knew more about the whereabouts of setts in his own part of the county than he did further afield. The figures set out in Appendix II are, in a sense, 'guesstimates'. And, as I have already pointed out, the distribution of badger carcases found on the roads and reported to MAFF can hardly be taken to represent a random sample of the distribution of all the badgers killed by cars or lorries.

Anomalies

66. It is necessary to refer briefly to what some critics of your Department's policies regard as 'anomalies' — that is to say, the occurrence of infected badgers' setts in the South West in the vicinity of dairy and beef herds that have not

suffered breakdowns, and also the fact that a few isolated infected badgers have been picked up in other parts of the country where no breakdowns have been reported.

67. I have already implied that one likely explanation for anomalies is that transmission of the disease is dependent on population density – that is to say, isolated groups of badgers might be infected in localities where they do not come into close contact with cattle. Equally, however, it needs to be remembered that different species not only vary in their susceptibility to the tubercle bacillus and in the form the disease takes, but that the members of a species, and indeed of any social group within a species, can be expected to vary in their resistance to infection. Not all, say, of ten people who are in the company of someone with a heavy cold will catch it; some may, some will not. So it is with all infections. When tuberculosis was widespread in the United Kingdom, it was not uncommon for one spouse to contract and die of the disease, while the other, who may have shared the conjugal bed for years, escaped unscathed. The Brontës are a classical case of TB affecting some but not all members of a family. The children Branwell, Emily and Anne all died of TB within eight months of each other. Charlotte died six years later, not of TB, but of 'excessive pregnancy nausea'. Their father died at the age of 84, as did Tabby the housekeeper, and no one ever supposed that it was TB that killed them. They had probably been mildly infected with the tubercle bacillus when young, and were subsequently immune.

68. What have been called 'anomalies' in the saga of the badger are as much the rule as the exception.

7 Other Considerations

Other Species

69. Although tuberculosis is all but unknown today in better-run zoos, many species of wild animal are known to be susceptible to tuberculous infection under captive conditions (see Appendix VI). Several critics of MAFF's policies have, not surprisingly, asked why only the badger has been made a 'scapegoat'. Why should the reservoir of the bovine tubercle bacillus not be some other species, say, the fox or the rat or the stoat? Why is it that the possibility of some reservoir host such as a biting insect, common to both badger and cow, has not been considered? These are all valid questions, even though they do not affect the basic fact that at least in the South West the badger is without question a harbourer of the bovine organism.

70. I have already referred to Dr. McDiarmid's observations on TB in wild animals, made over a span of nearly 40 years. His findings – in general, negative – are set out in Appendix I, Table 11.

71. In their investigation of herd breakdowns, MAFF officers have also arranged that a number of animals other than badgers should be examined. Their results have again, in general, proved negative (Appendix I, Table 12), as have routine examinations of animals submitted to, or collected by the MAFF Veterinary Investigation Centres (Appendix I, Table 13). Sheep and goats are very rarely – if at all – affected.

72. The negative results of a more recent study by Dr. Paul Barrow, while seemingly less impressive numerically than either of the two preceding series, are on the other hand very convincing. In addition to the badgers which MAFF officers were themselves collecting, Dr. Barrow collaborated with them in examining as many other wild mammals as could be trapped in two areas in the South West where outbreaks of TB in cattle had been associated with the presence of the disease in badgers. Bacteriological examination of the badgers was carried out at MAFF's Veterinary Investigation Centre in Gloucester, and using identical methods, Dr. Barrow, then at the London School of Hygiene and Tropical Medicine, examined all the other mammals that had been collected. He also tested the fleas, lice and ticks on the creatures he examined. His results are set out in Table 14 of Appendix I. However few the number of specimens for some of the species, it is highly significant that the badger was the only creature in the vicinity of the farms where breakdowns had occurred to reveal tuberculous lesions.

73. A general statement on the subject of TB in British wild animals has been provided for me by Mr. Gallagher of the Gloucester Veterinary Investigation Centre, and is reproduced in Appendix VII. It, too, tells the same story.

74. Experimental work has shown that some animals (for example, the rat) are very resistant to the tubercle bacillus. Several other creatures – woodmice and house-mice, rabbits, hares, hedgehogs, moles and even earthworms – have been examined, some by straightforward pathological and bacteriological study, some also by inoculation experiments, but no indication has emerged that any of these species plays a significant part in the epidemiology of TB in cattle. The rodent most commonly eaten by badgers is said to be the vole, of which 4,300 (collected in Wales, Southern England and Oxfordshire) were examined between 1936 and 1939. Not one was found to harbour the bovine tubercle bacillus, although a related strain, which has since died out, was found.

75. While the available evidence clearly implies that the badger is very vulnerable to the tubercle bacillus, it would help to meet the criticism that this animal has been made the scapegoat in the story of TB in cattle were surveys to be made systematically of all wild mammals that can be found on farms where herd breakdowns occur. To discover how vulnerable they are relative to the badger would, however, necessitate the testing of fairly large numbers. Simple probability calculations show that as many as 300 specimens would have to be sampled to pick up one positive if on average only one in a 100 in a given population were infected. If only one in a 1,000 was on average infected, the number that would need to be sampled is close to 3,000.

Other Factors

76. In addition to the suggestions that have been made that creatures other than the badger might be transmitting TB to cattle, or to both cattle and badgers, my attention has been directed to the possibility that poor husbandry may also be a factor contributing to herd breakdowns.

77. It stands to reason that some farmers are better than others. There must have been wide differences in the quality of animal husbandry in every county when the area-eradication programme was started in 1950. Farms then also had their cats and dogs, as they still do. There have always been rats, voles and rabbits on farms. Nonetheless, the fact is that the area attestation programme has succeeded everywhere except in the South West. It is surely illogical to suppose that the average standards of animal husbandry of farmers of the South West, acutely aware as they are of the problem of TB, are now worse than those of farmers in other parts of the country. Equally, the very small number of cowmen with tuberculosis, or the numbers of moles or rats that may be encountered on farms, cannot be the explanation for the fact that most herd breakdowns occur in the South West. These variables presumably are the same all over the country. I doubt whether any of these factors help explain the problem which I have been investigating.

Other Countries

78. The occurrence of tuberculosis in badgers had been reported in Switzerland before the condition was discovered in Britain. In the belief that the badger/cattle problem in other countries must necessarily be the same as in the

United Kingdom, the Dartmoor Badgers Protection League, an organisation which was formed in August 1979, approached the Irish, Danish, Swedish and French authorities to learn whether the badger is regarded as a reservoir of the bovine tubercle bacillus in their countries. The reply from Ireland, where the incidence of bovine TB is still comparatively high, referred to positive findings of the bacillus in wild badgers, but said that the animal was not regarded as a major factor in the spread of the disease in cattle. Although no tuberculous badgers had been reported in Denmark, the authorities there wrote that reservoirs of the disease in hosts other than cattle represented a permanent risk of reinfection. The Swedish reply was negative, as was the French.

79. The only comment that needs to be made about these observations is that they in no way invalidate what we know about the badger in this country. The argument that has been advanced by the Dartmoor Badgers Protection League, that because badgers in Denmark or France are not a reservoir of the bovine tubercle bacillus, and that consequently badgers in South West England are unlikely to be, would be akin to saying that because foxes in Great Britain are, happily, not a reservoir of rabies, it would be wrong to suppose that those of the European continent are carriers of this terribly dangerous virus – which, alas, they surely are.

8 Is Bovine TB something to worry about?

80. The justification for MAFF's policy of gassing badger setts which are, or which could be, involved in the transmission of bovine tuberculosis is that the Government is committed to preventing the spread of the disease in cattle. In the opening pages of this report I have referred to the background to this policy, and I have also briefly considered the connection between TB in cattle and TB in man.

81. Some critical observations of the Ministry's policy that have been made carry the implication that it is unnecessary to continue the campaign to suppress bovine TB. "Any suggestion that human health is at risk because of possible infected badgers", wrote the organisation called the Cotswold Wildlife Preservation Society, "is nonsense. Most retail milk is treated, and TB cattle are slaughtered". According to the Dartmoor Badgers Protection League, "the scare over danger to human health must be scotched from the outset – there is virtually no threat to humans of death from bovine TB and there has not been a threat for many years". This organisation's information was that on average only 100 people a year ("mostly immigrants") picked up bovine TB, and that only one died. Paradoxically, it annexed to its submission the letter it had received from the Danish authorities, and which pointed out that the bovine tubercle bacillus does cause TB in people, who can then pass the disease to cattle.

82. In 1977, the latest year for which official figures are available, 9,520 cases of TB in humans were notified in England and Wales, and 990 people died from the disease. The number who are infected by the bovine as opposed to the human tubercle bacillus is not known, since typing is no longer carried out except in selected cases. In 1977, 112 new cases due to the bovine bacillus were typed and, in 1978, 127. About one in 60 of all cases that were typed in 1978 turned out to be due to the bovine tubercle bacillus.

83. Some who have argued that bovine tuberculosis is no longer a threat to human health have suggested either that "nature should be allowed to take its course" with badgers and cattle, or that a 'cordon sanitaire' should be created to cut off the affected counties of the South West, or at least Cornwall, from the rest of the country. I do not propose to comment in any depth on these views, but I might make the following observations:

(a) With the exception of the South West, it took only some ten years to reduce the incidence of herd breakdowns to their present low levels. If the national eradication policy were now stopped, it could take no more time for the incidence of TB in cattle to rise to its previous level.

(b) It is in the highest degree unlikely that the cattle of the South West, numbering about a quarter of the total national herd of England and Wales, could be insulated from that of the rest of the country – or those in Cornwall from those in Devon.

(c) If bovine TB were allowed to flourish unchecked in the South West, diseased cattle would expose cowmen, farmers, and slaughterhouse workers and their families to a far higher risk of tuberculosis than they now run.

(d) The South West is 'tourist country', and while farmers in general are not allowed to sell direct to the public more than 50 gallons a year of the milk they produce, a certain number are licensed as producer-retailers who can dispose of all their untreated milk either directly or as cream and butter. In Cornwall alone, over 90 farmers are registered as producer-retailers. If the incidence of bovine TB in cattle were allowed to rise unchecked, not only would more human beings be at risk, but those affected would then become carriers of a disease which they could transmit to others.

84. There are several other powerful reasons – among them the agreed policy of the European Community to suppress bovine TB in the regulation of trade in livestock – why it is inadvisable for "nature" to be allowed "to run its course" in the epidemiology of bovine TB, either in the country as a whole, or in the South West in particular. In the final analysis, I cannot imagine legislators voting for the reversal of a public-health and animal-health policy which has already achieved so much, and whose economic importance is so obvious.

85. It is strange that those who oppose the Government's policy, either because they refuse to accept that badgers get TB, or because the elimination of the disease means that healthy as well as sick badgers are killed, seem to care little whether cattle contract the disease. Concern about cruelty to animals can be very selective.

86. A related criticism that has been made to me, both in writing and verbally, is that Government policy is of no value since the measures that were introduced in 1975 cannot stamp out TB in the whole population of badgers. This particular argument was advanced not only by those critics who hold that the disease in cattle is being taken too seriously, but also by others.

87. Obviously it will be difficult, if not impossible, to destroy every tuberculous badger. After all, it has not yet proved possible to eradicate the disease in man or in cattle. But this does not mean that an attempt should not be made to reduce the prevalence of the disease in the badger population. The world would be in a sorry state if measures that have been taken over the past century to eradicate other diseases had not been embarked upon without a prior assurance that they would be 100 per cent successful.

88. The policy that was being pursued by your Department until a standstill was declared on new gassing operations pending the outcome of my review, was to eliminate infected badger groups where it can be shown that their presence was associated with herd breakdowns. As I have said, I am satisfied that the reduction in the number of badgers up to the time of the moratorium was accompanied by a decline in the number of reactors in the herds concerned. Since on scientific grounds there is strong reason to posit a causal relation between the two events, the policy is justified. The policy would also be justified were it to result in a decline in the prevalence of the disease in badgers – although I should point out

that the submission sent me by the Cotswold Wildlife Preservation Society states that it is none of your Department's business to concern itself with the health of badgers.

89. The problem is not just the elimination of pockets of infection among badgers. Your officials have to try to prevent cleared setts from being recolonised from the periphery by a new lot of tuberculous animals, or by clean badgers which then contract the disease from viable bovine tubercle bacilli that may persist in decaying corpses, or in underground latrines, or in bedding. I shall return to this point later. But since the spread of tuberculosis is clearly density-dependent, both within species (as in man), or between species, it stands to reason that the eradication of TB in badgers will help contain the spread of the disease to cattle. What needs to be defined is a clear long-term strategy.

9 Criticisms of the measures taken against Badgers

90. Some criticisms of a more constructive kind than those that I have dealt with so far have been made by several bodies which accept that badgers are a secondary reservoir of the bovine tubercle bacillus, but who at the same time believe that badger control measures can be improved. Here I should particularly note the County Naturalist Trusts of the South West. Helpful comments have been sent to me by the Mammal Society, by the Nature Conservancy Council, by Dr. Kruuk, a member of the Institute of Terrestrial Ecology in Kincardineshire, who has spent several years studying the ecology of the badger, by Dr. Neal, a naturalist whose life-study has been the behaviour of the animal, and by Miss Eunice D. Overend, of the Wiltshire Trust for Nature Conservation.

91. In the light of the representations that have been made, the issues which I need to consider are:

(a) The number of badgers that have to be collected to determine whether they are the cause of a herd breakdown.

(b) The fact that short of a post-mortem, no test is available to tell whether a badger has TB.

(c) The way in which badgers are caught.

(d) The lack of a vaccine to cure TB in badgers or to safeguard them against it.

(e) The effectiveness of gassing.

(f) The number of setts which it is decided to gas, given a decision to clear an area.

(g) The large number of badgers which are killed relative to those found to be infected with the disease.

(h) The need to prevent recolonisation.

Number of Badgers Sampled

92. As I noted in paragraph 75, there is a simple statistical procedure for calculating how large a sample of a population suffering from a given disease would need to be surveyed to pick up one that is afflicted. If one animal in a 100 had the disease, at least a single positive should, on average, be encountered in a sample of 300. With a prevalence of one infected animal in ten, the corresponding figure would be 30. Everyone, however, knows that even if the chances of a coin coming down heads are one in two, the coin when flipped could, on occasion, fall tails 10 times in a row. Chance works like that.

93. I am informed that on average MAFF officials have sampled only five badgers per incident when it was suspected that these animals were the source of a

herd breakdown, but that on occasions where there was a high probability of badger involvement, far more had been collected for post-mortem study. In one instance, it was necessary to autopsy as many as 40 before the suspected 'positive' was found.

94. It is extremely unfortunate that there are times when very large numbers of badgers have had to be caught and killed in what is essentially a diagnostic process. But at the same time, I can see no other practicable way by which MAFF officials – with their operations monitored by the Consultative Panel and co-operating as they do with representatives of the Nature Conservancy Council – could have discharged the responsibilities that rest on their shoulders. Searching for 'contacts' in certain contagious human diseases can also prove a laborious business, even when it is possible to put direct questions and receive direct answers from, and to test, those who may be concerned.

The Diagnosis of TB in Badgers

95. Not surprisingly, however, some of the badger protection groups insist that instead of an autopsy, a method to diagnose the disease in the living animal "must" be devised. Unfortunately, no such method is anywhere within sight. The tuberculin test works in some mammals, but not in others, and the badger belongs to the latter group. There is another test ('enzyme-linked immunosorbent assay') to which some have referred, but which also does not work. It is known by the acronym ELISA, and whereas the tuberculin test is one that is applied to the tissues of the skin, the ELISA test uses blood serum. The difficulty here is that tuberculosis induces what is called 'cell-mediated immunity', and that the complicated responses of the tissues in reacting to a tuberculous infection are not reflected in the constituents of the serum. The Central Veterinary Laboratory has looked into the matter, using sera from 44 badgers, but with equivocal results. The same is true of other tests (e.g. 'complement-fixation') that have been tried. I have discussed this problem with two independent and distinguished immunologists, one connected with the World Health Organisation, but in the light of what I was told I decided that it would be an expensive waste of time to go on trying, even though Professor R. Canivenc of the University of Bordeaux, a French medical colleague whose work on the reproductive processes in badgers I have been following for many years, had offered me for further investigation the sera of over 100 badgers, which he had stored for a different purpose. In the course of more than 20 years of experimental research on the badger, the results of which are known to scientists the world over, Professor Canivenc has autopsied well over 1,000 specimens. He has noted several pathological conditions, but has never observed obvious tuberculous lesions, although he qualifies the information which he has provided me with the remark that he has never made a systematic search for the tubercle bacillus. At my suggestion, he tried the ordinary tuberculin test on 50 of the animals which he keeps in his laboratory, but none reacted. This was hardly surprising; even if badgers did react to the tuberculin test, his specimens had been caught in a part of France where bovine tuberculosis is practically unknown. He

has also inoculated two badgers with a culture of the bovine bacillus. These animals also failed to respond to the tuberculin test.

96. There is a point which I should make here. Those who 'demand' that a scientific test for bovine TB in badgers should be devised overlook the fact that were it possible to discover such a test, veterinary officials would be more than happy to use it rather than go through the laborious pathological and bacteriological procedures which they now have to follow.

97. But even if there were a test to replace present procedures, what then? In that case, I imagine that not just a small sample but, in the event of a herd breakdown, up to, say, 20 or more badgers would have to be trapped, tested and, if proved negative, then caged until the search for a reactor ended, or the search was abandoned. Once a reactor was found, every badger in every sett in the vicinity of the reactor would have to be captured, tested, killed if positive, and caged if not, until the whole operation was completed. All the caged animals would then have to be retested – as are cattle – new positives removed, and the captives held until they were all registered as free from disease. This is not a practical policy.

Are Badgers caught for test in the best practicable and most humane way?

98. The British are a nation of animal lovers. The Royal Society for the Prevention of Cruelty to Animals was launched in 1824, at a time when children were still sent down the mines; the National Society for the Prevention of Cruelty to Children (the NSPCC) was founded only in 1884, 60 years later. It may be irrational, but it is hardly surprising that there has been so much hostility to the idea that the badger, one of the best loved of the wild mammals of our countryside, should need to be controlled, or that complaints should be made about the cruelty that is associated with the capture and destruction of the animal.

99. The only three practicable ways that wild badgers can be captured in order to discover whether they have TB are shooting, trapping and snaring. No other method has been suggested to me. Being nocturnal, the animal (in the condition it would be required for examination) would not as a rule be an easy target for any but the best marksmen equipped with rifles furnished with special infra-red sights. Trapping seems less objectionable than snaring, which was the cause of the action for cruelty which, as I have already noted, was unsuccessfully brought against the Minister and one of his officials by Mrs. Murray who, while a protagonist of trapping, nonetheless admits that it, too, is cruel; as she has put it, the badger when trapped will, "for quite a time, explode with fear and aggression". Clearly the relative 'humaneness' of trapping and snaring will depend on the skill and consideration shown by the operator, especially in the frequency of the visits he makes either to traps or snares. MAFF officials who have caught badgers for subsequent release have found that the animal usually damages itself less frequently in a snare than in a cage-trap. They bite the mesh of the cage in trying to escape whereas, unless they are left unattended for too long, they usually accept restraint in a snare (whether it be round the neck or middle).

100. The less extreme groups from whom I have heard and with whom I have conferred, all agree that trapping is not practical policy. It would call for the presence of a watcher near the traps throughout the night. Unfortunately, the resources are just not available for this to be done.

101. I have neither snared nor trapped a badger, but am assured that a snare furnished with a swivel is humane. I have seen the corpse of one animal that had been illegally snared in a loop of smooth wire set in a barbed wire fence. The sight was indeed horrible. The upper part of the creature's trunk around which the snare had tightened was deeply lacerated. The person who removed the animal did not know how many days or hours had passed after it had been snared before it had been killed by a blow to the head.

102. What I learnt from the incident of the illicitly killed badger – I assume not a unique incident – is that however difficult the task, there is a danger that cruelty will become a more acute issue than it already is if the elimination of badgers is not controlled. That cannot be done by amateurs, however good their intentions, and however concerned they may be lest farmers, in trying to rid their land of badgers, "take the law into their own hands" – a phrase that has been used to me several times.

103. Enthusiastic animal lovers defeat the very purpose which concerns them if they make it difficult for Government officials to discharge their duty using approved methods of catching badgers. On occasion some have already prejudiced the situation by destroying traps set by MAFF officials. Battles between badger lovers and officials trying to carry out their duties must be avoided.

A Vaccine to protect Badgers?

104. The value of immunisation against TB with BCG, a vaccine made of attenuated but live tubercle bacilli, was once doubted — indeed is still doubted by some – but the general view now is that it has played, and is still playing, a powerful part in preventing a rise in the incidence of tuberculosis in the population of the UK. Every year Local Authorities in both England and Wales offer BCG vaccination to some 800,000 children in the thirteen-year age group. Those who take up the offer – about 650,000 – are first tuberculin tested. A small percentage respond positively, meaning that they have already been 'infected' by the tubercle bacillus. These children are therefore not given the vaccine, which is administered to the remaining 600,000. Several other European countries follow a similar regime. It has, however, been reported that an extensive experiment in Southern India with BCG has not proved successful, probably because the epidemiology of the disease is different there from what it is in Western Europe.

105. BCG vaccination of cattle has been tried in several countries, including the UK and France, but it has been found neither practical nor effective. In this country MAFF conducted two vaccination trials during the 1940s and 1950s, the results of which have not been widely published. The first trial ran for eleven

years and involved four herds of cattle which were known to have naturally-occurring bovine TB. Forty-seven tuberculin-test-negative calves were vaccinated at six-monthly intervals with BCG made from the bovine tubercle bacillus. At the end of the trial period 25 per cent of the vaccinated animals, and 50 per cent of their 'contacts', were found to have tuberculous lesions.

106. The second trial involved considerably more cattle, but did not last as long as the first, owing to the start of the area-eradication programme. Some 5,000 cattle in 73 herds were involved, and at the end of the trial, post-mortem examinations revealed that 30 per cent of the vaccinated animals, and 50 per cent of the non-vaccinated, had TB lesions.

107. As a result of these and other trials, notably in the United States and Canada, the international organisations concerned with livestock diseases, including the FAO and the WHO, now advise against BCG vaccination of cattle. Within the European Community the use of the vaccine is incompatible with the rules agreed by all the Member States governing intra-Community trade in livestock. These stipulate that programmes to eradicate bovine TB in cattle must be based upon the tuberculin test.

108. The suggestion has nonetheless been put to me that a vaccine should be devised which either cures TB in badgers, or protects them against the disease. Were such a search to be launched, its success could not be guaranteed. One can no more command a 'breakthrough' in immunology than in any other branch of science.

109. Furthermore, were such a vaccine discovered, its use would entail the same all but impossible process that I have just described for the application of a diagnostic test on the living animal.

110. I have already referred to the fact that many years ago it was discovered that the field vole, the young of which are eaten by badgers, may suffer from a form of tuberculous infection. One suggestion that has been put to me is that a vaccine for voles might be discovered, and that immunised voles could be introduced into badger country, in the hope that by consuming the voles, badgers might conceivably achieve some measure of immunity. Unfortunately for this suggestion, not only does it appear that the vole disease has died out, but the particular mycobacterium by which the creatures were afflicted in England was not the bovine variety. Unsuccessful attempts were made at that time to produce a vole vaccine which might be suitable for both men and cattle.

111. The susceptibility of the vole to the bovine tubercle bacillus is now being re-investigated in Sweden, but nothing of practical value has yet emerged from these new studies.

The Effectiveness of Gassing

112. Another matter of concern is the effectiveness of killing badgers by gassing

setts with cyanide. I raised this issue with the Consultative Panel, and specifically asked the representative of the RSPCA whether he knew of a better way of dealing with social groups of badgers suspected of being tuberculous. The answer was no. Nonetheless, I decided to enquire further and arranged a meeting with those members of the staff of the Government's Chemical Defence Establishment who are as well informed on the subject as are any people in the country.

113. The only likely chemical alternatives to cyanide are carbon monoxide and the nerve gases. The latter, however, are too dangerous to handle, and the former is, weight for weight, significantly less toxic than cyanide, and therefore likely to prove less effective than cyanide in practice. On the other hand, further enquiries about cyanide should, in my opinion, be made. For one thing, the speed with which cyanide gas kills at different concentrations, while known for a few species, has not been determined for badgers. We should find out what concentration in the air of the sett would be needed to kill quickly and humanely. Second, we should, if possible, discover a better way of disseminating cyanide gas throughout the tunnels and chambers of a sett than by blowing in particles of solid cyanide preparations, as at present. These are technical issues which only the experts can settle. Finally, there is the matter of timing. A question that I have been asked in the course of my enquiries is, how do Ministry officials know that all the members of a group of badgers suspected of harbouring the tubercle bacillus are 'at home' when gassing operations are started, and how can they be sure that 'suspects' do not escape during the course of such operations, to roam and spread the disease? The latter contingency would, of course, not arise were gassing carried out as effectively as it probably could be. But clearly the answer to the first question is that no one could ever be sure that all the members of a group were in their setts when gassing started. What we do know is that they would be more likely to be underground in the late autumn and winter; most foraging and fighting takes place at other times of the year. What is more, if the objective is to eliminate badgers suspected of harbouring and of transmitting the tubercle bacillus to their own kind, and of reducing the population of badgers, then the chances are that gassing would achieve the greatest success if carried out in the later winter months, when the animals (and their young) are most likely to be in their main setts during the day, and when efficient gassing would be helped by a prevailing higher humidity. This is something which I suggest should be carefully considered.

The Killing of Healthy Badgers

114. I propose considering this issue together with that of the arbitrary nature of the number of setts that are gassed once it is decided that a herd breakdown needs to be dealt with by the extermination of badgers and the prevention of recolonisation. This is clearly a matter for serious concern. But the question is, what can be done about it?

115. Badgers, like most wild animals, map their own world. The distribution of a species, the territories occupied by its members, the home range of a particular group or individual, even migratory patterns, are usually fixed in time and space.

Badgers are killed on motorways and roads because these cross home ranges which have been fixed geographically for longer than motor cars have existed. The swallows and house-martins hatched one year return, after a flight of thousands of miles, to the very eaves where they began their lives. The boundaries of the Serengeti National Park do not delimit the migrations of vast numbers of game animals for which the Park was to be a sanctuary; the animals were not asked how the map of the Park should be drawn, any more than badgers indicate in advance what will be the limits of the home range in which they propose to live.

116. Dr Cheeseman and Mr Mallinson, two MAFF field-workers who have been engaged in a detailed study of badgers in Gloucestershire, have found that the members of a social group occupy a discrete territory, the boundaries of which are covered by well-defined tracks. The greater the local population of badgers, the more densely packed are the social group territories, with increased chances of contact between badgers of neighbouring social groups. In this field experiment – which is similar to one that has been carried out by French workers – the movements of many members of 28 social groups have been followed for some four years by means of radio-tracking devices, infra-red binoculars, and by mapping badger distribution by laying bait containing coloured plastic markers which are subsequently found in the badger latrines (see Appendix VIII). The same two workers have reported abnormal behaviour in badgers when in the terminal stages of tuberculosis. They may wander in seemingly disorientated fashion well outside their normal home range – even to the extent of making some farm building their final refuge. Diseased badgers may also wander into the territory of neighbouring setts, so spreading infection.

117. Once it is decided that diseased badgers are the most likely cause of a herd breakdown, the setts to be gassed are mapped by MAFF officials who have carried out surveys following guidelines that have been approved by the Consultative Panel. Each case is treated on its own merits, taking into account the likely interaction of neighbouring social groups of badgers, and the fact that one group might make its home in two or even more adjacent setts. In areas with a small population of badgers which roam more widely, it is conceivable that in some cases too few setts have been treated. In others, it is possible that too many setts have been gassed. If the number of setts that are occupied by an infected social group of badgers is not known precisely, it is however inevitable that the decision about the number that should be gassed will to some extent be arbitrary. Another difficulty arises from the fact that farm boundaries do not necessarily delimit the home range of a group of badgers, as is made only too clear in a letter from a Wiltshire farmer, reproduced in Appendix III (No.7). A further problem is illustrated by the well-known incident in which 'protesters' made it impossible for MAFF officials to gas setts on common-land which was part of the home range of a social group of badgers that had been identified as possible contacts of an infected badger found after a breakdown on an adjacent farm. But quite apart from the matter of boundaries, it is always necessary to bear in mind the problem of the solitary or sick badger, wandering into farm buildings, or into the territory of some neighbouring group, either doing this because it has been ejected from its own, or has become disorientated, and spreading infection as it goes.

118. I share the concern of those who fear that too many badgers may be destroyed in the course of dealing with a particular herd breakdown. I am disturbed by the fact that gassing will destroy not only those badgers which have already been infected by the tubercle bacillus, but also some that have not yet contracted the disease. But given a programme to eliminate badgers infected with TB, and since it is not practicable to deal with individual animals in isolation, I cannot, for reasons that I have already outlined, see how it could be arranged that only diseased badgers should be killed. But I would hope that in time it should be possible to decide more precisely than is possible at present the location of the setts used by one social group of badgers, and also those of any interlocking sett or setts – and particularly those, some of whose inhabitants, whether healthy or diseased, may start recolonising gassed setts.

10 Summing Up

119. I have not been asked to judge the moral issues which could be said to be involved in the policy of killing badgers in order to protect cattle – and, at further remove, ourselves – from tuberculosis. Nor shall I attempt to judge whether one approved method of trapping or snaring is more humane than another. Having so far concentrated on such criticisms of a precise kind as have been made of your Department's actions, what remains is to consider whether the realisation of MAFF's objectives could be made more assured than appears to be the case now.

Factors which determine the Numbers and Distribution of Badgers

120. The national survey of active setts that was organised by the Mammal Society with the help of County Naturalist Trusts provides a background for some very detailed studies that have been made by Dr Kruuk of the factors that determine the size and distribution of social groups of badgers in Scotland. These both extend and complement earlier studies which he made in Wytham Woods near Oxford, and also the detailed findings of Dr Cheeseman and Mr Mallinson in the enquiry on which they are engaged in the Cotswolds.

121. As is only to be expected, badgers are found only in terrain where it is possible for them to dig setts, where they can find cover and in areas where they can forage for food. Although the animal is an omnivore, extensive analyses of the creature's droppings made by several workers, including Dr Kruuk, have shown that about half of the food it normally consumes consists of earthworms – a point which Professor Canivenc has also noted in the area of France where he has worked. These are caught at night on pasture and in deciduous woodlands. The animal avoids fields with long grass and relatively low worm densities. In the laboratory, badgers can thrive and breed on artificial diets, for example, one consisting predominantly of day-old chicks.

122. The size and composition of groups, and the extent of the area over which they range, are determined by their territorial relationships and by the availability of nutrient. Dr Kruuk has described one family party made up of 14 individuals, but the usual number is closer to eight, with sexually mature females usually outnumbering males. He has also reported groups made up of males only. The area which constitutes the home range of one 'clan' studied by Dr Kruuk in northern Scotland measured as much as 1,500 hectares (3,707 acres). In the lusher Oxford area, where he began his investigations, the average size of a group's territory was only about 90 hectares. The home range of the groups under investigation in Gloucestershire is as little as 25 hectares as compared with about 75 in Cornwall.

123. While gassing operations have eliminated some groups of badgers, the available information makes it plain that MAFF's operations in no way threaten the survival of the species in the United Kingdom. Indeed, those who can speak with authority on the subject hold that the total population of badgers, numbering well in excess of 100,000, was increasing until a few years ago. Some say that it has since remained steady; others that it is still on the increase – partly because of conservation legislation, and also because of the break-up of large estates and the decline in the numbers of gamekeepers. Given no disastrous and widespread epidemic of disease, the reproduction rate of the badger, even taking into account the high mortality rates of cubs, is sufficient to assure the viability of the species in these islands. Nor is there any suggestion that the badger is threatened on the European continent, in parts of which the animal is regarded and treated as a pest so as to prevent its excessive multiplication and to reduce the damage it does to crops. The badger is widely distributed all over France where, in spite of being systematically hunted by hunting organisations (Fédérations de Chasse), it is in no danger of extinction, partly because it also lives in inaccessible areas.

The Spread of Disease

124. Many factors may be involved in the interchange of the tubercle bacillus between badger and badger, or between badger and calf or cow, but it would be flying in the face of scientific reason not to recognise the part played by population density. A small group of badgers foraging over an area of 1,500 hectares containing relatively few cattle in which the prevalence rate of TB is very low – if indeed the disease is there at all – is in a different world from one living in a tenth of that space together with herds of cattle which are subject to breakdown. It is not just what we know about the badger that points to this conclusion. The story of the New Zealand possum leads to the same general proposition. In short, more badgers and more cattle mean greater opportunity of contact and easier spread of communicable disease. As Dr Neal has pointed out, conditions in the South West, such as in the Cotswold escarpment, and the rich pastures and mild climate of Cornwall, not only favour animal husbandry, but also encourage the multiplication and spread of badgers. In these parts of England the range size of a social group is smaller than in areas where there are fewer badgers, and boundary fights are correspondingly more frequent.

125. Thus, in contrast to what has happened as man's standard of living has improved, the nutritional advantages which badgers enjoy in the South West, as compared, say, with badgers in the north of Scotland, have conduced to high population density in an area where both they and cattle harbour the tubercle bacillus. It seems obvious that no indecisive strategy is going to eliminate the disease in the badger population. Moreover, so long as badgers in the South West constitute a significant reservoir of the bovine tubercle bacillus, the culling of infected cattle, without a parallel decrease in the population of badgers, is not likely to have much effect on the incidence of herd breakdowns. Here it is relevant to refer to views expressed by Dr Neal about the relationship between the population-density of badgers and the incidence of tuberculosis. In a

report published by the RSPCA, he is quoted as saying.

"The badger unit is a social group and when there are a lot of badgers, the social groups are in close proximity and their territories are small. They can survive because the feeding within these territories is adequate, or apparently so. But because the territories are condensed, there is much more aggression between the badgers of separate territories. In a moorland district there is no problem at all, as the question of territory hardly arises because the area is so large. But in parts of Gloucestershire an area perhaps as small as 100 acres serves a social group, which spends the whole of its life there. The youngsters of the group possibly at a year old, move out to find territories of their own if the social group cannot absorb them. . . So you've got the situation of considerably increased aggression in areas of high density and one of the factors which has frequently come out in recent discussions with the Ministry is that TB is passed from badger to badger often by actual bite wounds received during territorial combats. In this manner the disease may spread more rapidly."

126. No one knows all the factors that are involved in the epidemiology of tuberculosis. As Professor T. McKeown has observed, the history of the disease in the United Kingdom makes it plain that the number of human deaths for which it was responsible, and correspondingly its prevalence, were on the decline before the introduction of BCG vaccination or of effective antibiotic treatment. Indeed, mortality was already falling sharply at the time when the disease first became notifiable about the middle of the nineteenth century. The general view is that our own increased resistance to tuberculosis came about because of improved living conditions – such as better and less crowded housing and more fresh air – and in particular of better nutrition, and that as the fall continued, fewer people ran the risk of cross-infection. The decline in human TB caused by the bovine bacillus was, of course, essentially due to the elimination of tuberculous cattle and to the pasteurisation of milk.

127. Tables 15 and 17 of Appendix I suggest that both the extent of infection amongst badgers and the form the disease takes may have changed as a result of the gassing programme. There are also indications of seasonal variations in the incidence of TB in the animal, in parallel with a normal physiological cycle which reveals itself in variations in body-weight and thyroid activity. (As a normal event, adult sows lose weight in spring and summer, while the male badger loses on average about half its body-weight (by the early summer).

128. Unfortunately, however, the disease in badgers is certainly not on the decline in some parts of the South West. Nine per cent (91) of 986 badgers that were collected in the affected areas and which were autopsied and studied at MAFF Veterinary Investigation Centres in the period January 1978 to 30 September 1979 were tuberculous. These figures are the best there are as indicating the improvement that had occurred in 1976 to 1977, that is to say over the preceding period of gassing (15 per cent — 191 of 1,231 badgers). In the seven months to 30 April 1980, following the suspension of new gassing operations in September 1979, 207 more badgers from the affected counties have been autopsied. Twenty-nine i.e. 14 per cent, were found to be tuberculous. Over the

same period the percentage of positives in the large samples that came from Gloucestershire and Avon has jumped from seven-and-a-half to 19 (Appendix I, Table 18).

129. Some of the animals that were autopsied in the Veterinary Investigation Centres of the South West during the seven months concerned may, of course, have died before the moratorium on gassing was imposed and their carcases may have been refrigerated and kept for later examination. This qualification does not, however, imply any bias in the figures since this kind of delay has apparently always applied because of shortage of staff. There can be no doubt, therefore, that there has been a significant increase in the incidence of the disease in badgers since last October, and it is a disturbing thought that tuberculosis may now be spreading from the dense, highly-infected population in the South West to badgers in contiguous counties. At the same time, however, it should be noted that the figures in Table 19 of Appendix I do not provide any indication of a parallel increase over the period in the incidence of herd breakdowns in the areas concerned. The figures about breakdowns which I now have do not lend themselves to any conclusion since information is not available about the timing of tuberculin testing during the relevant months.

130. What is abundantly clear, therefore, is that the problem into which I have been enquiring concerns not only tuberculous cross-infection between cattle and badgers, but – and regardless of the gassing programme – the future of the badger itself. By any epidemiological standards the prevalence of the disease in the badgers of the South West is dangerously high. Overall, since 1971 it has been found in nearly 15 per cent of some 4,000 animals from the affected areas (Appendix I, Table 12). What the figures imply is that at least one in five to one in ten badgers in these areas is now infected with TB. One in four of 144 dead badgers that were picked up in fields, woods and farm buildings – that is to say, animals that were not road casualties – between 1972 and 1978 in Gloucestershire, Avon and Wiltshire, were found on autopsy to be tuberculous (Appendix I, Table 16). Tuberculosis is clearly a very significant cause of natural death in badgers in parts of the South West.

131. The disease obviously flares violently in pockets, as it once did in the human population, and as it did in cattle before the TB eradication programme was started 30 years ago. Contrary to an interpretation that has been put to me by a leading member of the Wiltshire Trust for Nature Conservation, the concept of pockets of infection does not mean that the badger population throughout the country may not be affected by a low level of tuberculous infection, or that stray tuberculous badgers will not be found between infected setts, a factor in the spread of infection. Nor, given the now incontrovertible evidence that the prevalence rate of TB is dangerously high, does it mean that gassing operations in the South West should be limited in scope because gassing might disrupt social groups, leaving the survivors to wander, spreading disease.

132. What it does mean is that operations to eliminate badgers suspected of harbouring the bacillus should be more effective than they are now, and that it is not unlikely that a high proportion of all wandering badgers in areas where the

40

disease is rampant are carriers of the TB germ. It also means that, however difficult, steps should be taken to prevent recolonisation of gassed areas. We are dealing with a TB prevalence rate in the badgers in parts of the South West that has already reached extremely dangerous proportions – not with a series of minor outbreaks.

133. In the light of what we now know, man and cattle on the one hand and cattle and badgers on the other can be regarded as having constituted interchanging reservoirs of the main types of the tubercle bacillus that affected the health of all three species before measures were taken to control tuberculosis. One can speculate that badgers all over the country once suffered and died of the disease at least as frequently as did cattle and their human contacts, and that the prevalence of the disease in badgers declined over the country as a whole in parallel with its decline in the human and cattle populations. But now that two links – man and cattle – in this chain of infection and transmission are under control, it is the badger alone which in the South West, where there are very high concentrations of both cattle and badgers, plays a significant part as a continuing reservoir of the disease. Cattle there now act as 'sentinels' for the badger, in the same way as the canary in the coal-mine once indicated dangerous concentrations of gas. The occasional appearance of the disease in cattle reflects a high local prevalence of TB in badgers.

134. Unfortunately, what we do not know is how one pocket of infection in badgers relates to another. I have asked whether the TB one finds in the badgers of Gloucestershire has any connection with the disease as it occurs in Cornwall, or whether the animals of these two counties have been infected independently by cattle (on the assumption, which I am ready to accept, that cattle gave the disease to the badger, and not the other way round). No one knows the answer. The topography of Great Britain does not lend itself to the clear conclusion which the New Zealand authorities were able to draw about the possum – that separate pockets of infection by cattle of possums were, and are still, occurring.

135. Another difficulty is that it is impossible to make generalisations about what level of infection in an animal that is a reservoir of a dangerous bacillus or virus could be regarded as tolerable from the point of view of transmission to other hosts. The level would depend on a variety of local factors. For example, in one part of Gloucestershire that has been closely studied, where the density of badger groups is high and home ranges correspondingly smaller, the incidence of TB, while still high (about 30 per cent) was nonetheless lower than in social groups of badgers of Cornwall which on average lived in, and roamed, larger areas. What has to be remembered too is that in the case of some diseases, for example rabies, one single outbreak would have to be contained in the most vigorous way possible, and that whole herds of cattle have had to be sacrificed to prevent not only the spread of foot-and-mouth disease but also of TB itself.

136. In short, we simply do not know what level of TB infection in badgers could be regarded as 'safe' either from the point of view of the spread of tuberculosis between badger groups, taking into account differences in population densities, or from badgers to cattle. I have discussed this question with medical and

veterinary colleagues with experience of the spread of infectious diseases, and it has been put to me that since there can be no *a priori* answer to the question, and since the present level of infection in the South West is very high by any epidemiological standards, the only thing that must be done is to set about reducing the prevalence of the disease in badgers as rapidly as possible.

137. Such a policy would be greatly helped if we knew what the present rates of infection were in the counties which ring the more highly-infected parts of the South West, and where sporadic cases of tuberculosis in badgers have already been identified. If only in the interests of fauna preservation, I would therefore suggest that a determined effort be made now to discover what the infection rate is in the badgers of, say, Hereford and Worcester, Wiltshire, Somerset, Devon, Dorset and Hampshire.

138. Given the information that such sampling would provide, it should be possible to proceed to a more reliable, even if still empirical, way of judging what level of infection in badgers could be tolerated, both from the point of view of the spread of infection within the species and that of cross-infection with cattle. In the ideal what is wanted is some yardstick which would make it possible to correlate the incidence of breakdowns in herds to indices of badger population density and associated levels of infection, standardised for the distribution and size of farms carrying cattle, and of the localisation of badgers in the areas concerned.

139. Where the evidence points to badgers as the source of a herd breakdown in areas where the animals are known to be heavily infected, gassing operations are unlikely to achieve their purpose if all setts that may be involved are not treated, and if repopulation is not prevented. The eradication policy has clearly succeeded when it has been applied to large areas (Appendix III), whereas in some instances it has clearly not had the desired effect. The 'flexibility' that now characterises decisions about the extent of a gassing operation needs to be monitored by officials who learn all that is known about the movement of badgers from local farmers and others who may be concerned, and who are also fully conversant with the kind of information about the overlap of home ranges that is being gathered in Scotland under the aegis of the Institute of Terrestrial Ecology, and in Gloucestershire by MAFF officials. The more the ecologists who are working on the subject are brought into the act, the better. Half-measures, or measures taken without an understanding that the situation we are facing is a TB epidemic of serious proportions in badgers, are not going to succeed, any more than half-measures would have succeeded in reducing the prevalence of TB in the cattle population.

140. In summary, having reflected hard on some views that have been put to me. I have come to the conclusion that the problem is not going to be solved by gassing fewer rather than more suspected setts in any given operation within heavily-infested areas. Since the ideal, however unrealisable, would be to create a 'no-man's-land' across which no badger, whether healthy or unhealthy, could pass into a cleared area, I would also suggest that whenever a gassing operation is carried out, land-engineers and soil scientists should be consulted about ways to

make cleared setts uninhabitable, and how to prevent new setts being constructed within cleared localities. Needless to say, a careful watch should always be kept in areas where gassing operations are carried out for solitary or wandering badgers that might have been displaced.

141. In the knowledge that dense populations of badgers conduce to the spread of the disease, Dr Kruuk has suggested a novel approach to the problem of thinning them out. What he proposes is that pastures in affected areas should be so dressed as to reduce drastically the population of earthworms which they sustain. This, he suggests, would not only reduce the availability of a staple item of their diet, but would also make the animals forage more in woodland and shrubland on the edge of fields, so reducing the chance of their coming into contact with cattle. I do not know whether there is a way of doing this without detriment to the cattle which also forage the pastures that would be treated. Nor do I know what those concerned with the welfare of birds – which also eat worms – would think about the measure that Dr Kruuk has proposed.

Translocation

142. Some people have suggested that badgers should be moved from areas where TB is rife to cleaner localities, and I am informed that this has been done on occasion. Translocation, as it is called, however, carries a risk that badgers that are moved may already be infected – this situation was narrowly averted in one proven case. Since no test short of an autopsy can determine whether a badger is healthy or tuberculous, the practice is dangerous. In my view, steps should be taken to prohibit people, whatever their motives, from taking and moving badgers in areas known to have significant rates of infection – say, one per cent. There is another aspect to this problem. The fact that the disease has now become very common in the badgers of the South West means a real risk of its transmission, not only to cattle, but also to those individuals in that part of the country who, for whatever reason, decide to keep the animals as pets.

The Human Problem

143. Even when they are adamant in rejecting what to any informed scientist would be irrefutable fact, the groups most hostile to MAFF's policy are insistent that they are not 'crackpot extremists'. The fact is that opposition costs protesters little or nothing – any price that has to be paid is exacted in time by officials, in pounds and pence by the farmer and taxpayer, and in health by the badger. Moreover, concern for the animal – whether healthy or tuberculous – is matched by what could be regarded as a cynical attitude to matters which concern the public health, as well as by a general belief that whatever Government officials do is necessarily misguided.

144. This kind of reaction also constitutes a fact, as much a fact as does the existence of TB in the badger.

145. While I have no experience in these matters, it seems to me that the public

reaction against the killing of badgers that are believed to have been the cause of herd breakdowns is largely due to a failure of communication, and of a consequent widespread ignorance. Whether this failure can be put right, I do not know. But if it is to be, it is clearly essential that the people who live in the affected counties should be better informed than they now are of the reasons for the Government's policy.

146. With hindsight one can also recognise a failure of communication within governmental circles. Officials working in the affected areas know that there is a serious TB epidemic in badgers in the localities which are their responsibility, but so far as I can judge this has not been matched by a sufficient awareness at the centre of the need to publicise the facts. Were news of the existence of TB in badgers broadcast without qualification as it emerges, even the most sentimental conservationist would surely demand that vigorous steps should be taken to halt the spread of an epidemic which, while a serious hazard to the farmer, also threatens the local survival of the badger. The chances of TB infection occurring in badgers in the affected areas now range from about one animal in five to one in ten. Since badgers live in small social groups, infection in any one member is likely to spread to the lot. And infection will spread from group to group. This is the essence of the problem which I, a dedicated scientific conservationist, now have to recognise.

147. The Consultative Panel was set up not only to help MAFF in the execution of its policy, but also to serve as a link between the Ministry, conservation bodies, and the RSPCA. I have met the members of the Panel and am confident that it is a useful body which should remain in being. I say this even though I recognise that the word of the Panel now carries little weight with some organisations that have set themselves up as protection societies – but amongst whom I failed to find any professional biologists, medical men, or veterinarians who have examined the evidence which I have collected and reviewed in this Report.

148. Clearly it is too much to expect that the members of the Panel should undertake a public relations task in a regular and sustained way; they all have other duties and affairs to which they must attend. I would therefore suggest that the County Naturalist Trusts which are concerned, and which recognise the value of the Panel – even if some are critical about the secrecy of its deliberations – should appoint officers to liaise with MAFF's veterinary staff in the South West. It would be the responsibility of these liaison officers to keep their membership informed about what is being done in their counties. Those appointed for this task should be competent to transmit to people who are ready to listen an understanding of the medical, veterinary and ecological aspects of the whole problem. The basic issue which MAFF needs to put across is that tuberculosis is a serious disease both in man and cattle, and that badgers have become significant carriers of the disease. The task will take time, effort and money, but I do not anticipate any cooling of the heat which the subject of the badger now engenders unless something positive is done to improve public relations.

149. I have discussed this idea with your Department's Regional Veterinary Officer in the South West, and am assured that from his point of view there

would be no difficulties in its implementation. I have also put the suggestion to members of the Naturalist Trusts whom I met, and they too would be willing to co-operate. The self-appointed protection and pressure groups with whom I discussed the matter were not interested. Nor would I expect them to be before the facts of the situation are properly revealed.

150. What is regarded as unjustifiable secrecy on the part of MAFF about areas of infection with which it proposes to deal only intensifies suspicion. Of course, I do not know what those who protest about secrecy had in mind to do had they been informed of the whereabouts of herd breakdowns, and about the considerations which might lead the Ministry's officials to the conclusion that badgers are the cause of a herd breakdown. Those whom I have met do not claim the kind of scientific understanding of the epidemiology of bovine tuberculosis that would be needed were they to try to check the reasoning behind any programme of action that might be decided by Ministry officials. But informed publicity should help put this right.

151. At the same time I can well understand why farmers are chary about broadcasting news of breakdowns in their livestock, and why they have been supported in this attitude by both the NFU and by MAFF. Whether or not a breakdown is regarded as a reflection on the standard of a farmer's husbandry, it certainly affects his finances. In the case of beef cattle, a standstill after a breakdown means that until the herd once again satisfies the tuberculin test replacements cannot be brought in or animals moved off except for immediate slaughter. This inevitably implies a reduction – sometimes a lengthy one – in cash flow. Tuberculous dairy herds also imply a financial loss, even though the milk produced can still be disposed of to the Milk Marketing Board.

152. But whatever the reasons either for or against the maintenance of secrecy, the establishment of a responsible link between farmers, MAFF officials, and naturalist groups should help satisfy rational doubters that what the 'Ministry Men' propose to do in containing a breakdown is at least 'above board'. At the same time, a freer exchange of information about breakdowns between MAFF officials and veterinarians would provide a warning to those in private practice to be on the lookout for trouble on farms which come under their care, and which are in the vicinity of others where breakdowns have occurred and where badgers are the likely cause.

153. But – and I repeat – a great deal of the public reaction against your Department's policies derives from a general lack of understanding of the dangers of tuberculosis. The fairly widespread belief – that it is an unimportant disease – is a consequence of its relative rarity today both in man and cattle. People forget that diseases which have been partly eradicated can easily return given any relaxation of the measures that have helped bring about their decline. There is also little understanding of the fact that levels of so-called natural immunity fall as diseases disappear. The fact that TB was on the decline – in the human population certainly, and possibly also in cattle — before the introduction of modern diagnostic and therapeutic measures which are now available to deal with the disease, does not mean that we could risk the

abandonment of tuberculin testing, or of BCG vaccination, or of antibiotic treatment.

154. The basic and incontrovertible fact is that TB in badgers is now a significant secondary reservoir of the disease in parts of the South West, dangerous for badgers and cattle alike. Given the policy to suppress bovine TB, the disease cannot be allowed to spread in the badger population. Short of a fundamental change in the Government's policy for the suppression of bovine and human TB, I cannot therefore see any reason for continuing the moratorium on the campaign to eliminate tuberculous badgers. As I have already said, I am confident that the Ministry's policy does not constitute a threat to the survival of the species in the United Kingdom. Indeed, the very high prevalence of tuberculosis in the badgers of the South West seems to me to be a far greater threat, for if the disease were to take hold in badgers in other areas of the country, there is no saying what the consequences would be, not only so far as the transmission of TB to cattle is concerned, but also as they relate to the survival of the badger in our country.

11 Recommendations

155. In the knowledge

(a) that in some parts of the South West of England something like one in five to one in ten badgers has tuberculosis and that by any rational epidemiological standards badgers now constitute a significant reservoir of the bovine strain of the tubercle bacillus (paragraphs 45 and 130);

(b) that the disease seems to have spread since control measures were halted in October 1979 (as, for example, in Gloucestershire), (paragraph 128);

(c) that in comparison with the rest of the country, the affected counties are the home of disproportionately large numbers of both badgers and cattle (paragraph 60);

(d) that because population-density is a major factor in the spread of TB, conditions in presently-affected areas not only favour the transmission of the disease from badgers to cattle, but from one infected group of badgers to another (paragraph 60);

(e) that herd breakdowns already occur much more frequently in these areas of the country than elsewhere (paragraph 8);

(f) that in spite of the prevalence of TB, the nutritional and environmental conditions of the South West favour the multiplication of badgers (paragraph 125); and

(g) that whereas control operations of the kind that were carried out in the South West in relation to herd breakdowns at no time constituted a threat to the survival of the species nationally, but that the spread of TB among badgers now implies a major hazard to their survival (paragraphs 123, 129 and 130);

I recommend

(i) that control operations in the affected areas, including gassing, be resumed as soon as possible, and that they continue to be monitored not only to discover what effect they have on the outbreak of TB in cattle but, in addition, and equally important, on the prevalence of the disease in badgers (paragraph 154);

(ii) that an effort be made to discover how prevalent TB is in the badgers of counties contiguous with the areas now affected (paragraph 137);

(iii) that experts from the Government's Chemical Defence Establishment be called in to devise improvements in the gassing procedures that have been used hitherto (paragraph 113);

(iv) that steps be taken to reduce the length of the interval that separates a decision that badgers are involved in a herd breakdown from the start of control operations (paragraph 42);

(v)   that in addition to badgers which are suspected of being associated with a herd breakdown, other wild creatures should be systematically sampled and examined for TB (paragraph 75);

(vi)   that the actual timing of individual gassing operations be carefully controlled (paragraph 113);

(vii)   that the public in all parts of the country be reminded of the need to inform Ministry officials of road-casualties or of the presence of dead badgers either in woodland, pasture, or farm-land, so that they can be taken for examination to the State Veterinary Centres (paragraph 63);

(viii) that land-engineers and other scientists who might have ideas relevant to the problem should be consulted by MAFF officials about measures to prevent recolonisation of cleared setts and localities (paragraph 140);

(ix)   that the Consultative Panel on Badgers and Tuberculosis be kept in being to act as a central forum of advice (paragraph 147);

(x)   that in the counties affected, officers be appointed by the County Naturalist Trusts to liaise with the Ministry's veterinary staff with the responsibility of keeping themselves informed about official operations against badgers, and of communicating with interested conservation groups (paragraph 148);

(xi)   that in the affected counties there should be a freer exchange of information about herd breakdowns between MAFF veterinary staff and veterinary surgeons in private practice (paragraph 152);

(xii)   that in the hope that knowledge so gained will help in all aspects of the control programme, field-work on the behaviour of badgers in general should continue to be encouraged, in the same way as decisions about the extent of gassing operations should take into account all that can be learnt locally about the movement of badgers (paragraph 139);

(xiii) that no badgers which live in areas where the prevalence of TB is as high as it now is in parts of the South West be moved to other areas; that is to say, that 'translocation' be forbidden (paragraph 142); and

(xiv)   that (a) interim reports of the progress of the control programme should, if possible, be published annually; and (b) that an overall review should be conducted at the end of three years and its results published, with its focus on changes in the prevalence rate of tuberculosis in badgers, as well as on the numbers of herd breakdowns.

156. In March 1979, six months before the moratorium on gassing operations was imposed, the Government stated that it expected the scale of gassing to decline as outbreaks of TB in cattle in the control areas of the South West fell to the average level which applied in the rest of the country. In my view this goal is too theoretical. Instead, I would suggest that the Ministry's objective in the affected areas should be to lower the prevalence of TB in the badger population by selectively reducing their numbers to whatever level experience will in due course show is of no significance either to the problem of cross-infection with cattle, or as a threat to the local survival of the species in the South West.

Appendices

APPENDIX I

Table 1: Number of cattle reacting positively to the tuberculin test, 1961-79

Year	Great Britain (i) Total no. of cattle in herds tested	(ii) Total no. of reactors	(iii) Incidence of reactors (%)	South-west England (i)	(ii)	(iii)	Cornwall (i)	(ii)	(iii)	Gloucestershire (a) (i)	(ii)	(iii)
1961	9,230,473	14,984	0.162	1,671,678	4,177	0.250	257,042	1,545	0.601	183,498	535	0.292
1962	9,005,775	9,780	0.108	1,719,447	3,366	0.196	314,328	1,345	0.428	189,879	442	0.233
1963	8,637,280	5,901	0.068	1,629,363	1,572	0.096	305,516	674	0.221	181,545	215	0.118
1964	8,041,584	5,128	0.063	1,622,706	1,822	0.112	328,467	751	0.229	187,155	199	0.106
1965	7,546,460	3,463	0.046	1,493,686	1,171	0.071	328,028	569	0.173	173,565	148	0.085
1966	7,141,192	3,248	0.045	1,490,795	1,364	0.091	322,735	424	0.131	190,068	347	0.185
1967	6,253,889	3,047	0.049	1,444,185	1,398	0.097	307,803	493	0.160	184,157	406	0.220
1968	5,854,915	2,170	0.037	1,422,058	1,037	0.073	284,910	504	0.177	201,404	232	0.115
1969	5,793,648	2,418	0.042	1,304,784	1,135	0.087	326,765	653	0.200	194,754	204	0.105
1970	5,049,790	2,081	0.045	1,201,640	1,240	0.103	311,174	724	0.233	183,385	155	0.085
1971	4,771,848	1,834	0.038	1,105,011	1,216	0.110	319,016	719	0.225	158,586	155	0.098
1972	4,519,210	1,568	0.035	1,121,982	1,068	0.095	293,312	682	0.233	159,034	94	0.059
1973	4,962,572	1,574	0.032	1,128,475	1,179	0.104	319,301	653	0.204	165,222	320	0.193
1974	4,818,534	1,624	0.034	1,336,374	1,125	0.081	360,983	537	0.146	150,512	167	0.110
1975	4,412,134	1,666	0.038	1,097,568	1,160	0.098	322,902	506	0.156	136,961	209	0.152
1976	3,984,171	1,058	0.027	1,066,336	787	0.068	274,654	222	0.081	138,768	210	0.151
1977	3,857,119	764	0.020	1,082,512	533	0.046	256,927	159	0.062	127,223	93	0.075
1978	3,593,630	668	0.019	980,650	468	0.044	217,437	189	0.096	136,620	89	0.065
1979	3,478,362	628	0.018	968,407	346	0.036	166,511	128	0.077	123,344	34	0.028

Note

(a) As from 1 April 1974, boundary changes have resulted in a reduction in the total area of this county.

Table 2: TB infection rates in cattle herds in England, Scotland and Wales, 1972-78

	No. of cattle herds recorded at June 1975 Agric. Census	No. of herds infected 1972-78	No. of herds infected per 1000 herds
England	110,287	925	8.4
Northern	15,679	49	3.1
Yorks & Lancs	14,333	15	1.0
E Midlands	12,052	17	1.4
W Midlands	19,549	66	3.4
Eastern	7,450	11	1.5
S Eastern	11,521	21	1.8
S Western	29,703	746	25.1
Wales	26,879	59	2.2
Scotland	25,352	115	4.5
Highlands	5,393	3	0.6
North East	8,058	48	6.0
East Central	3,075	29	9.4
South East	1,961	19	9.7
South West	6,865	16	2.3
Total	162,518	1,099	6.8

Table 3: Bovine TB in badger carcases (mainly road casualties) reported to MAFF laboratories by members of the public; 1 January 1976 — 30 April 1980

	No. of badger carcases submitted	No. of carcases from which *M. bovis* isolated
ENGLAND		
Avon	101	2
Cornwall	303	8
Devon	145	6
Dorset	48	0
Gloucestershire	232	21
Somerset	60	0
Wiltshire	73	3
Total South West	962	40 (4.2%)
Bedfordshire	3	0
Buckinghamshire	11	0
Berkshire	9	0
Cambridgeshire	24	0
Cheshire	12	0
Cumbria	4	0
Derbyshire	25	0
East Sussex	28	0
Essex	13	0
Hampshire	24	0
Herefordshire	38	1
Hertfordshire	2	0
Kent	30	0
Lancashire	2	0

51

	No. of badger carcases submitted	No. of carcases from which *M. bovis* isolated
Leicestershire	22	0
Lincolnshire	17	0
Northamptonshire	10	0
Northumberland	5	0
Nottinghamshire	3	0
North Yorkshire	5	0
Oxfordshire	12	0
Shropshire	16	0
Staffordshire	10	1
Suffolk	1	0
Surrey	33	3
Tyne and Wear	4	0
Warwickshire	41	0
West Midlands	2	0
West Sussex	12	0
West Yorkshire	1	0
Worcestershire	20	0
Total rest of England	439	5 (1.1%)
Total England	1,401	45 (3.2%)
SCOTLAND		
Border Region	2	0
Inverness	2	0
Lothian	1	0
Stirling	1	0
West of Scotland	1	0
Total Scotland	7	0
WALES		
Clwyd	5	0
Dyfed	106	0
Glamorgan	9	0
Gwent	18	0
Gwynedd	4	0
Powys	22	0
Total Wales	164	0
Total Great Britain	1,572	45 (2.9%)

Table 4: TB history of cattle on a Dorset farm where gassing of badger setts began in August 1975

Year	No. of tuberculin tests	Average no. of animals tested	No. of reactors slaughtered	No. of cattle with visible lesions of TB
1955	1	173	0	0
1956	1	235	0	0
1957	1	230	0	0
1959	1	276	0	0
1960	1	312	0	0
1961	1	237	0	0
1962	1	226	0	0
1963	1	286	14	6
1964	1	216	1	0
1965	1	483	0	0
1966	1	431	1	1
1967	1	389	0	0
1968	1	377	0	0
1969	1	429	0	0
1970	2	450	134	66
1971	3	377	13	9
1972	2	426	6	0
1973	2	550	45	18
1974	4	505	138	33
1975	5	479	61	32
1976	3	539	6	0
1977	2	524	6	0
1978	1	549	0	0
1979	1	511	0	0

Table 5: TB in badgers on a Dorset farm where gassing of setts began in August 1975

Year	Carcases examined for *M. bovis*		Faeces examined for *M. bovis*	
	Positive	Negative	Positive	Negative
1973	–	–	–	–
1974	11	6	12	46
1975	12	3	6	14
1976	1	15	–	22
1977	–	9	–	15
1978	–	8	–	14
Total	24	41	18	111

Table 6: Prevalence of TB in cattle in the Thornbury Experimental Area (North), 1966-1979

Year	No. of animals	No. of herds tested	No. of herds with reactors	Total no. of reactors (VL + NVL)
1966	1,675	23	3	3
1967	1,697	22	6	15
1968	1,278	16	4	5
1969	1,960	24	0	0
1970	1,778	23	1	1
1971	1,832	22	1	2
1972	1,959	24	0	0
1973	1,876	22	0	0
1974	2,324	25	2	2
1975	1,827	21	2	9
1976	2,195	21	3	11
1977	2,453	25	1	1
1978	2,324	25	0	0
1979	2,116	22	0	0

(VL = Visible lesions of TB; NVL = No visible lesions of TB)

Table 7: Prevalence of TB in cattle in the Thornbury Experimental Area (South), 1966-1979

Year	No. of animals	No. of herds tested	No. of herds with reactors	Total no. of Reactors (VL + NVL)
1966	6,391	89	0	0
1967	6,159	86	5	26
1968	6,352	84	7	73
1969	8,069	93	7	9
1970	9,844	114	12	16
1971	8,443	108	4	7
1972	9,454	109	3	13
1973	8,701	98	11	37
1974	12,010	115	22	79
1975	10,492	99	15	23
1976	10,412	102	7	12
1977	9,353	113	9	13
1978	10,435	115	2	3
1979	10,010	107	0	0

(VL = Visible lesions of TB; NVL = No visible lesions of TB)

Table 8: TB history of cattle on Raftra and Ardensawah farms, Cornwall, where gassing of badger setts began in November 1976

RAFTRA

Year	No. of tuberculin tests	No. of I/Rs	No. of Reactors	Post Mortem VL	Post Mortem NVL
1956	1	1	0	0	0
1959	2	3	1	1	0
1964	1	0	24	21	3
1965	2	0	11	4	7
1967	1	1	0	0	0
1969	1	0	4	1	3
1970	2	4	0	0	0
1971	1	0	1	0	1
1973	2	0	3	2	1
1976	1	1	0	0	0
1977	1	1	0	0	0
1978	1	0	3	3	0
1979	1	0	1	1	0

ARDENSAWAH

Year	No. of tuberculin tests	No. of I/Rs	No. of Reactors	Post Mortem VL	Post Mortem NVL
1958	1	1	1	N/A	N/A
1959	2	2	1	N/A	N/A
1960	2	6	0	0	0
1961	1	9	0	0	0
1962	1	0	1	1	0
1964	1	2	0	0	0
1965	3	1	10	0	10
1966	3	7	2	1	1
1967	1	6	0	0	0
1968	3	2	30	8	22
1969	2	1	1	1	0
1970	2	2	2	0	2
1971	3	0	22	15	7
1972	3	0	31	15	16
1973	3	2	11	3	8
1974	3	6	1	0	1
1975	1	2	0	0	0
1978	2	1	1	0	1
1979	1	1	0	0	0

I/R = Inconclusive reactor
VL = Visible lesions of TB
NVL = No visible lesions of TB
N/A = Not available

Table 9: TB in badgers on Raftra and Ardensawah farms, Cornwall, where gassing of setts began in November 1976

Year	Carcases examined for *M. bovis*		Faeces examined for *M. bovis*	
	Positive	Negative	Positive	Negative
1972	6	} 32	1	} 2
1973	16		2	
1976	1	0	0	0
1978	0	4	0	0
1979	1	2	0	1
Total	24	38	3	3

Table 10: Source of TB infection in all infected cattle herds in England, Scotland and Wales, 1972-1978

	SOURCES OF INFECTION						
	Badgers	Imported Irish Cattle	Unknown	Purchased	Contiguous premises	Human	Other
Gloucester and Avon	198	2	54	12	0	0	0
Cornwall	51	0	234	37	18	0	0
Wiltshire Devon Somerset Dorset Sussex	82	2	53	12	2	0	0
Rest of GB	0	171	105	40	17	5	4 (a)
Total GB	331	175	446	101	37	5	4

Note
(a) 1 infected pig; 1 contaminated drinking water; 1 cesspit cleaning equipment; 1 cesspit contamination.

57

Table 11: Wildlife examined for TB by Dr A.McDiarmid, 1968-1979 at the Agricultural Research Council's Institute for Research on Animal Diseases, Compton

Species (a)	No. examined	Microscopic evidence of TB	Cultural examination
Deer 　Red 　Fallow 　Sika 　Roe	800	3	*M. avium* isolated from the 3 clinical cases; *M. avium* also isolated from 187 ileo-caecal lymph nodes from apparently normal deer.
Brown hare	300	–	*M. avium* isolated from 4.
Hedgehog	12	–	*M. avium* isolated from 1.
Grey squirrel	240	–	
Field vole	234	–	
Rabbit	20	–	
Rat	6	–	
Stoat	2	–	
Weasel	1	–	
Wild goat	1	–	
Fox	4	–	
Badger (b)	3	–	
Mole	10	–	
Total	1,633 (b)		

Notes

(a) Apart from the deer samples, several of which came from Scotland, most of the specimens came from England.

(b) Between 1944 and 1967 Dr McDiarmid also examined some 40 badgers from the counties of Oxfordshire, Berkshire and Hampshire. None was found to harbour the causative organism, *M. bovis*.

(c) In the footnote to his table, reproduced above, Dr McDiarmid commented:

"Apart from these more recent findings many different species have been examined for tuberculosis over a period of 20 years prior to 1968. The numbers could be well in excess of those recorded for the last decade in the above Table but precise details have not been kept. Suffice it to say that during my research career from 1940 to 1980 I have never seen a case of bovine tuberculosis in any free-living wild species in this country, and as Hon. Veterinary Adviser to the Game Conservancy and the British Deer Society, for many years, my opportunities to examine wildlife for disease have probably been better than most".

Table 12: Wildlife examined by the State Veterinary Service in connection with official investigations 1 January 1971-31 December 1979.

Species (viscera except where shown otherwise)	No. examined	No. found to be harbouring *M. bovis*	
Badger	4,011 (a)	563 (a)	(14.0%)
— Faeces	5,704	142	(2.5%)
Fox	339	3	(0.9%)
— Faeces	42	—	
Deer (Fallow, Sika & Roe)	16	—	
— Faeces	42	—	
Rat	291	5	(1.7%)
Rabbit	108	—	
Hare	8	—	
Grey squirrel	141	—	
Hedgehog	14	—	
Mole	80	2	(2.5%)
Mink	15	—	
Stoat	26	—	
Vole (field & bank)	752	—	
Shrew	69	—	
Polecat	1	—	
Weasel	12	—	
Woodmouse	540	—	
Mouse (other species)	159	—	
Cat	5	—	
Ferret	1	—	

Note
(a) Excludes badgers recorded in Table 3

Table 13: Animals other than badgers submitted for diagnostic purposes to MAFF Veterinary Investigation Centres by members of the public and practising veterinary surgeons, 1975-79 (a)

Species	No. examined		No. positive for *M. bovis*	
	Carcases	Viscera	Carcases	Viscera
Dog (b)	365	1,181	0	0
Cat (b)	292	262	0	0
Deer	87	104	1	0
Fox (c)	228	6	0	0
Hedgehog	29	0	0	0
Vole	67	0	0	0
Mole	15	0	0	0
Stoat/Weasel	9	0	0	0
Rabbit (d)	4,340	0	0	0
Rat/Mouse (d)	1,689	0	0	0
Squirrel	30	2	0	0

Notes

(a) These figures also include animals other than badgers collected by MAFF scientists in connection with research projects, but they exclude any animals collected in connection with official investigations by MAFF (see Table 12).

(b) 1977-79

(c) In 1973-4, 340 foxes were examined at the Carmarthen Veterinary Investigation Centre and all proved negative for *M. bovis*.

(d) Includes both feral and laboratory animals and, in the case of rabbits, animals kept for meat production.

Table 14: Results of examinations carried out by Dr P. Barrow in connection with a Nature Conservancy Council project on the identification of pathogenic mycobacteria in badgers and other wildlife

Animal Species	No. examined (a)	No. found to be harbouring *M. bovis*
Fox	12	0
Field Mouse	68	0
Rat	30	0
Vole	32	0
Shrew	10	0
House Mouse	7	0
Mole	17	0
Weasel	5	0
Rabbit	17	0
Grey Squirrel	20	0
Badger	56 (b)	14 (b)
Arthropod Parasites and Hosts		
Badger — fleas	137	0
lice	222	0
tick	1	0
Rat fleas	61	0
Field mice fleas	16	0
Mole fleas	6	0
Shrew fleas	2	0
Squirrel fleas	20	0
Fleas (Hosts not recorded)	43	0

Note

(a) All the samples were taken from 2 areas in Gloucestershire and Avon where known outbreaks of TB in cattle had been associated with the isolation of *M. bovis* from badgers living in the immediate vicinity.

(b) The badgers were examined at MAFF's Veterinary Investigation Centre in Gloucester using identical techniques to those used by Dr Barrow at the London School of Hygiene and Tropical Medicine for the other species. These badgers are therefore also included in the MAFF figures in Table 12.

Table 15: Badger carcases from all sources tested for TB at MAFF's Veterinary Investigation Centre in Gloucester, 1971-1979

Year	No. of Badgers examined (a)	No. of Badgers infected	Prevalence of infection (%)
1971	20	4	20.0
1972	94	21	22.3
1973	175	35	20.0
1974	253	50	19.8
1975	337	59	17.5
1976 (b)	443	84	19.0
1977	491	62	12.6
1978	551	56	10.2
1979	549	46	8.4
Total	2,913	417	14.3

Note

(a) All the badgers came from the counties of Gloucestershire, Avon and Wiltshire.

(b) Badger control measures started.

Table 16: TB in badger carcases picked up in fields, woods and farm buildings in Gloucestershire, Avon and Wiltshire (excludes road casualties and those killed in clearance operations), 1972-1979

Year	Badgers which died of natural causes – no. examined	No. of natural deaths due to TB	Natural deaths due to TB (%)
1972/75	60	24	40
1976 (a)	24	9	37
1977	53	11	20
1978	31	3	10
1979	26	7	27
Total	194	54	28

Note

(a) Badger control measures started.

Table 17: Severity of Bovine TB in infected badgers examined at the Gloucester Veterinary Investigation Centre, 1972-1979 (a)

Year	Visceral lesions (lungs, kidneys, etc) (%)	Lymph-node lesions (%)	Non-visible lesions (%)
1972-75	50	30	20
1976 (b)	23	10	67
1977	30	30	40
1978	10	50	40
1979	39	17	44

Note

(a) All the badgers came from the counties of Gloucestershire, Avon and Wiltshire.

(b) Badger control measures started.

Table 18: TB in badgers as determined by autopsies carried out by the State Veterinary Service to determine the source of infection in cattle

COUNTY	1976			1977			1978			1 JAN 1979 – 30 SEPT 1979			1 OCT 1979 – 30 APRIL 1980		
	No. Examined	No. Positive	%	No. Examined	No. Positive	%	No. Examined	No. Positive	%	No. Examined	No. Positive	%	No. Examined	No. Positive	%
Glos/Avon	373	78	20.9	439	58	13.2	245	28	11.4	275	21	7.6	95	18	18.9
Cornwall	83	11	13.3	102	20	19.6	141	18	12.8	108	14	13.0	82	7	8.5
Devon	43	2	4.7	41	11	26.8	43	6	14.0	31	1	3.2	17	0	–
Dorset	17	1	5.9	9	0	–	11	0	–	28	0	–	1	0	–
Somerset	4	0	–	0	0	–	16	0	–	23	1	4.3	0	0	–
Surrey (a)	0	0	–	11	0	–	20	1	5.0	0	0	–	5	0	–
Sussex (East) (a)	2	0	–	20	1	5.0	43	3	7.0	22	2	9.1	8	0	–
Sussex (West) (a)	1	0	–	14	2	14.3	4	0	–	0	0	–	0	0	–
Wiltshire	68	6	8.8	52	4	7.7	27	0	–	38	2	5.3	12	4	33.3

(a) Followed earlier history of infection in cattle.

Table 19: Number of herds in England and Wales with cattle reacting positively to the tuberculin test, January 1974 — March 1980

County	1974			1975			1976		
	Total no. of herds with reactors	No. of herds tested	%	Total no. of herds with reactors	No. of herds tested	%	Total no. of herds with reactors	No. of herds tested	%
South West England									
Avon	32	756	4.2	60	1,372	4.4	65	1,367	4.8
Cornwall	254	5,597	4.5	252	4,605	5.5	139	4,353	3.2
Devon	27	4,496	0.6	30	3,446	0.9	43	4,233	1.0
Dorset	15	1,427	1.1	23	1,036	2.2	6	1,142	0.5
Gloucestershire	76	1,967	3.9	99	1,669	5.9	87	1,879	4.6
Somerset	4	2,463	0.2	20	2,071	1.0	11	1,902	0.6
Wiltshire	13	1,296	1.0	23	830	2.8	34	1,108	3.1
Total South West	421	18,002	2.3	507	15,029	3.4	385	15,984	2.4
Rest of England									
Bedfordshire	0	188	–	0	156	–	0	99	–
Berkshire	2	245	0.8	1	206	0.5	2	184	1.1
Buckinghamshire	0	475	–	1	399	0.3	1	399	0.3
Cambridgeshire	0	427	–	2	374	0.5	0	149	–
Cheshire	0	168	–	18	1,759	1.0	9	1,245	0.7
Cleveland	0	0	–	1	105	1.0	0	94	–
Cumbria	6	3,077	0.2	17	2,625	0.6	12	1,934	0.6
Derbyshire	4	1,226	0.3	13	825	1.6	1	1,368	0.1
Durham	0	938	–	2	735	0.3	1	447	0.2
East Sussex	3	733	0.4	3	341	0.9	2	480	0.4
Essex	2	528	0.4	0	471	–	0	346	–
Hampshire	2	839	0.2	4	735	0.5	1	859	0.1
Hereford	0	223	–	8	1,106	0.7	4	1,052	0.4
Hertfordshire	0	245	–	0	231	–	1	155	0.6
Humberside	4	536	0.7	6	424	1.4	3	402	0.7
Isles of Scilly	0	0	–	0	0	–	0	0	–
Isle of Wight	1	144	0.7	0	117	–	0	117	–
Kent	2	555	0.4	2	545	0.4	1	579	0.2
Lancashire, Gt Manchester, Merseyside	5	2,150	0.2	21	2,790	0.8	5	1,232	0.4
Leicestershire	0	543	–	2	479	0.4	0	712	–
Lincolnshire	2	771	0.3	3	675	0.4	2	761	0.3
Norfolk	5	484	1.0	3	377	0.8	0	286	–
North Yorkshire	6	4,675	0.1	6	2,155	0.3	4	2,024	0.2
Northamptonshire	0	458	–	2	391	0.5	3	288	1.0
Northumberland	5	955	0.5	9	941	1.0	11	664	1.7
Nottinghamshire	0	331	–	3	455	0.7	2	334	0.6
Oxfordshire	1	550	0.2	0	469	–	0	424	–
Shropshire	12	2,002	0.6	5	1,203	0.4	6	1,631	0.4
South Yorkshire	0	0	–	0	241	–	1	343	0.3
Staffordshire	8	2,052	0.4	8	1,171	0.7	2	1,113	0.2
Suffolk	1	529	0.2	1	612	0.2	2	238	0.8
Surrey	0	244	–	5	349	1.4	2	416	0.5
Tyne and Wear	0	0	–	0	44	–	0	27	–
Warwickshire	2	} 740	0.3	7	654	1.1	3	478	0.6
West Midlands	0	}		0	96	–	1	103	1.0
West Sussex	0	405	–	10	422	2.4	2	405	0.5
West Yorkshire	0	0	–	3	848	0.4	2	890	0.2
Worcestershire	5	705	0.7	7	699	1.0	1	450	0.2
Total Rest of England	78	28,141	0.3	173	26,225	0.7	87	22,728	0.4
Total England	499	46,143	1.1	680	41,254	1.6	472	38,712	1.2
Wales									
Clwyd	2	1,295	0.2	3	1,253	0.2	2	974	0.2
Dyfed	22	4,169	0.5	56	3,580	1.6	13	3,915	0.3
Glamorgan	4	679	0.6	1	604	0.2	4	550	0.7
Gwent	1	684	0.1	2	487	0.4	1	371	0.3
Gwynedd	0	1,679	–	2	1,586	0.1	2	1,293	0.2
Powys	4	1,869	0.2	2	1,947	0.1	3	1,402	0.2
Total Wales	33	10,375	0.3	66	9,457	0.7	25	8,505	0.3
Total England & Wales	532	56,518	0.9	746	50,711	1.5	497	47,217	1.1

1977			1978			JAN-SEPT 1979			OCT 1979-MARCH 1980		
Total no. of herds with reactors	No. of herds tested	%	Total no. of herds with reactors	No. of herds tested	%	Total no. of herds with reactors	No. of herds tested	%	Total no. of herds with reactors	No. of herds tested	%
38	1,351	2.8	16	1,205	1.3	12	883	1.4	24	1,632	1.5
91	4,113	2.2	94	3,515	2.7	57	1,860	3.1	48	3,624	1.3
33	4,027	0.8	22	3,808	0.6	13	2,585	0.5	10	4,582	0.2
10	1,087	1.0	13	1,027	1.3	9	866	1.0	7	1,472	0.5
50	1,792	2.8	38	1,751	2.2	13	1,305	1.0	22	2,013	1.1
9	2,012	0.4	9	1,956	0.5	4	1,630	0.2	6	2,706	0.2
15	1,171	1.3	9	992	0.9	4	725	0.6	9	1,382	0.7
246	15,553	1.6	201	14,254	1.4	112	9,854	1.1	126	17,411	0.7
1	98	–	2	130	1.5	1	79	1.3	0	116	–
1	158	0.6	0	171	–	0	138	–	1	200	0.5
0	236	–	0	334	–	0	299	–	0	500	–
1	193	0.5	0	227	–	0	182	–	0	262	–
4	1,419	0.3	4	1,081	0.4	3	951	0.3	3	1,524	0.2
0	72	–	0	94	–	0	89	–	0	109	–
2	1,861	0.1	1	1,701	0.1	0	1,251	–	1	2,338	0.0
2	1,224	0.2	0	781	–	0	445	–	0	1,247	–
0	288	–	2	457	0.4	2	304	0.7	1	504	0.2
8	603	1.3	3	513	0.6	1	413	0.2	0	731	–
0	383	–	1	309	0.3	0	239	–	0	403	–
0	601	–	0	516	–	0	533	–	0	915	–
6	827	0.7	5	942	0.5	1	449	0.2	3	867	0.3
0	142	–	1	197	0.5	0	133	–	0	225	–
3	401	0.7	1	422	0.2	2	310	0.6	0	603	–
0	0	–	0	0	–	0	0	–	0	0	–
0	51	–	1	85	1.2	0	25	–	0	46	–
3	595	0.5	2	554	0.4	0	485	–	0	823	–
2	1,605	0.1	3	1,665	0.2	2	1,001	0.2	1	1,916	0.1
2	559	0.4	0	377	–	0	450	–	1	806	0.1
4	524	0.8	0	618	–	1	505	0.2	0	898	–
0	322	–	0	541	–	1	489	0.2	0	715	–
3	2,052	0.1	2	1,900	0.1	1	1,387	0.1	0	2,410	–
0	199	–	1	297	0.3	1	240	0.4	0	368	–
9	1,154	0.8	8	803	1.0	3	504	0.6	0	623	–
1	245	0.4	0	371	–	0	296	–	0	387	–
0	463	–	0	413	–	0	324	–	0	581	–
2	1,205	0.2	4	1,090	0.4	7	1,098	0.6	4	1,857	0.2
0	272	–	0	250	–	0	225	–	0	410	–
0	1.288	–	1	1.179	0.1	7	910	0.8	3	1,709	0.2
2	347	0.6	0	387	–	2	220	0.9	0	419	–
0	339	–	0	368	–	0	277	–	0	434	–
0	47	–	0	43	–	0	25	–	0	39	–
0	609	–	0	411	–	0	352	–	0	611	–
0	107	–	0	58	–	0	61	–	0	106	–
2	433	0.5	1	373	0.3	1	354	0.3	0	541	–
1	795	0.1	0	807	–	0	490	–	0	1,002	–
3	588	0.5	6	566	1.1	0	348	–	0	684	–
61	22,305	0.3	49	21,031	0.2	36	15,881	0.2	18	27,929	0.1
307	37,858	0.8	250	35,285	0.7	148	25,735	0.6	144	45,340	0.3
0	1,174	–	1	1,151	0.1	0	745	–	0	655	–
19	3,949	0.5	3	2,732	0.1	5	2,390	0.2	5	1,810	0.3
1	688	0.1	4	733	0.5	1	469	0.2	0	346	–
0	624	–	1	567	0.2	0	354	–	0	286	–
0	1,305	–	0	1,347	–	0	881	–	0	609	–
5	1,951	0.3	2	1,553	0.1	0	1,022	–	0	737	–
25	9,691	0.3	11	8,083	0.1	6	5,861	0.1	5	4,443	0.1
332	47,549	0.7	261	43,368	0.6	154	31,596	0.5	149	49,783	0.6

APPENDIX II

Estimated number and density of badger setts in the counties of England, Scotland and Wales (prepared by Mr E D Clements of the Mammal Society)

County	Estimated no. of setts	Average no. of setts per 1,000 acres
England		
Avon	500	1.5 (b)
Bedfordshire	250	0.8
Berkshire	300	1.0
Buckinghamshire (a)	650	1.4
Cambridgeshire (a)	180	0.2
Cheshire (a)	400	0.7
Cleveland	250	1.7
Cornwall	1,400	1.6 (b)
Cumbria	1,200	0.7
Derbyshire	700	1.1
Devon (a)	2,000	1.2 (b)
Dorset (a)	1,200	1.8 (b)
Durham	450	0.7
Essex (a)	500	0.6
Gloucestershire	1,200	1.8 (b)
Greater London (a)	150	0.4
Greater Manchester	70	0.2
Hampshire	600	0.6
Hereford and Worcester	1,050	1.1
Hertfordshire	350	0.9
Humberside	370	0.4
Isle of Wight	100	1.1
Kent (a)	900·	1.0
Lancashire	350	0.5
Leicestershire	500	0.8
Lincolnshire	400	0.3
Merseyside	20	0.1
Norfolk (a)	110	0.1
Northamptonshire	500	0.9
Northumberland	1,200	1.0
Nottinghamshire	300	0.6
Oxfordshire	350	0.5
Salop	600	0.7
Somerset (a)	1,500	1.8 (b)
Staffordshire	500	0.7
Suffolk (a)	260	0.3
Surrey (a)	500	1.2
Sussex, East (a)	1,550	3.5 (b)
Sussex, West	450	0.9
Tyne & Wear	150	1.1
Warwickshire	450	0.9
West Midlands	50	0.2
Wiltshire	900	1.0
Yorkshire, North (a)	1,000	0.5

County	Estimated no. of setts	Average no. of setts per 1,000 acres
Yorkshire, South (a)	250	0.6
Yorkshire, West (a)	250	0.5
Scotland		
Border	1,050	0.9
Central	300	0.5
Dumfries & Galloway	1,100	0.7
Fife	280	0.9
Grampian	1,150	0.5
Highland	620	0.1
Lothian (a)	500	1.2
Orkney	0	0
Shetland	0	0
Strathclyde	1,300	0.4
Tayside	550	0.3
Western Isles	0	0
Wales		
Clwyd (a)	650	1.1
Dyfed	1,500	1.1
Gwent	350	1.0
Gwynedd	400	0.4
Mid Glamorgan	130	0.5
Powys	1,050	0.8
South Glamorgan	70	0.7
West Glamorgan	200	1.0

Note

(a) Fairly well-recorded counties

(b) These high-density counties are probably under-estimated, whilst some of the low-density counties are probably over-estimated.

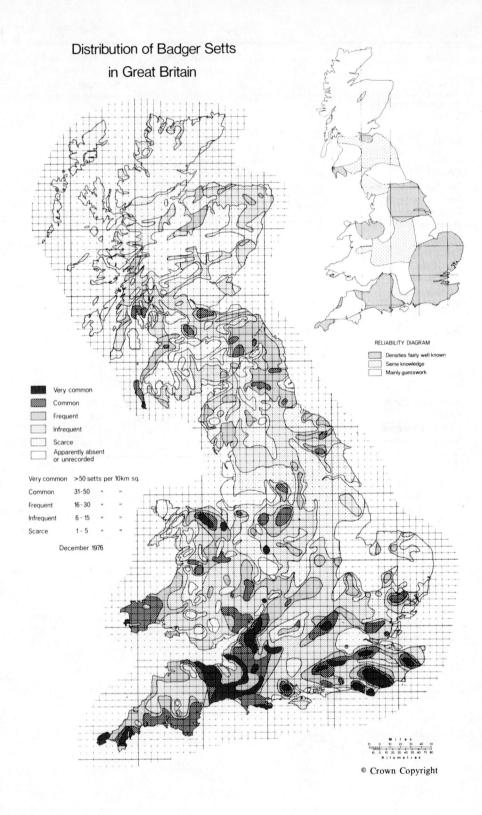

Distribution of Badger Setts
in Great Britain

RELIABILITY DIAGRAM

Densities fairly well known
Some knowledge
Mainly guesswork

Very common
Common
Frequent
Infrequent
Scarce
Apparently absent
or unrecorded

Very common	>50 setts per 10km sq.	
Common	31 - 50	" "
Frequent	16 - 30	" "
Infrequent	6 - 15	" "
Scarce	1 - 5	" "

December 1976

Miles
Kilometres

© Crown Copyright

68

Distribution of cattle herds infected with tuberculosis
in England, Scotland and Wales from 1972 to 1978
indicating origins of infection
(excepting the South Western Region)

Badgers •
Irish cattle ∆
Unknown ○
Contiguous premises ▲
Purchased animals ·
Human ♦
Miscellaneous ■

For distribution in this region
see separate map

Kilometres
0   50   100

Prepared and Drawn by Survey Section, Ministry of Agriculture, Fisheries and Food. © Crown Copyright 1979.

69

Distribution of the cattle herds infected with tuberculosis in the
South Western Region from 1972 to 1978, indicating origins of infection

Badgers   ●
Irish cattle   △
Unknown   ○
Purchased animals   ·
Contiguous premises   ▴

There are no human and miscellaneous
outbreaks in the South Western Region

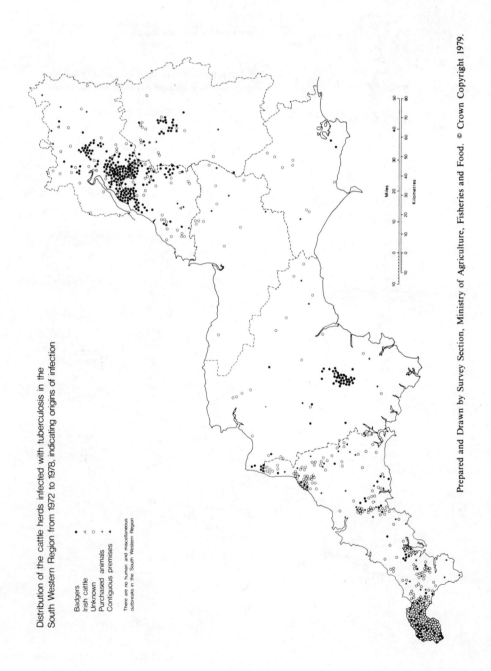

Prepared and Drawn by Survey Section, Ministry of Agriculture, Fisheries and Food. © Crown Copyright 1979.

APPENDIX III

The occurrence of TB in badgers in relation to herd breakdowns in South-west England

1. Dorset

Between 1956 and the final quarter of 1970 routine tuberculin testing of the cattle on a large farm in Dorset generally gave clear results (Appendix I, Table 4). A few animals reacted positively in 1963, 1964 and 1966, but after these had been slaughtered, the herd again tested clear. In 1970 a major outbreak of TB occurred. 134 reactors had to be slaughtered, of which 66 were found to have tuberculous lesions: when examined *post-mortem*. MAFF's investigations failed to establish the origin of infection. The herd tested clear in October 1971, and there were no further reactors until October 1972, when six marginally-positive reactors were slaughtered. These animals did not reveal visible lesions.

The next breakdown was in November 1973 when 45 cattle were slaughtered. The subsequent testing history of the herd is set out in Table 4 of Appendix I.

An enquiry by MAFF's veterinary staff into the origins of the massive breakdown in November 1973 revealed no evidence which linked it directly to the previous outbreak, and since recently-purchased stock and neighbouring herds had had clear tests, cross-infection from cattle seemed unlikely. It was noted that there were badgers on the farm, and these were investigated as a possible source of infection. The bovine tubercle bacillus (*M. bovis*) was cultured from faeces samples that were sent for laboratory analysis in January 1974. In June 1974, two badger carcases were submitted for examination. Both revealed extensive lesions of TB from which *M. bovis* was recovered. The results of the badger investigations are given in Appendix I, Table 5.

Since the herd's reactor rate remained at a very high level a badger-clearance operation was set in hand. At first, cage traps were used, but after the amendment in August 1975 of the law prohibiting the use of poison gas, gassing of setts was started and continued until May 1978. As indicated in Table 4, the number of cattle which reacted positively declined significantly from then on. *Post-mortem* examination of the 12 cattle taken for slaughter in 1976 and 1977 did not reveal tuberculous lesions and laboratory analysis failed to isolate *M. bovis*. There have been no further reactors since then.

A statistical analysis of the data collected from this location indicates cattle on the farm were at greatest risk of infection in the months of April and May, the beginning of the grazing season. This is of particular significance since work done at the MAFF Veterinary Investigation Centre in Gloucester has demonstrated that it is at this time of year that the incidence of bovine TB in male badgers is at its peak. The period from mid-February onwards is one of great stress in the male badger's yearly cycle. Range marking and fighting between rival males reach a peak in the Spring, increasing the chances of infection spreading from badger to badger and on to cattle.

71

2. Thornbury, Avon

An experimental badger-clearance programme in an area of some 10,000 ha near Thornbury was started in December 1975. There had been a long history of herd breakdowns in this area, and between 1966 and 1976 "visible-lesion reactors" had been found in no fewer than 39 herds (see Appendix I, Tables 6 and 7). Tuberculous badgers had been found in the area and a survey in the summer of 1975 revealed some 440 setts of which about a half appeared to be occupied. Of the 98 badgers submitted for *post-mortem* examination between 1972 and October 1975, 16 were found to be infected with bovine TB.

Gassing of setts started in December 1975, and by the end of August 1976, 177 had been treated. Many of these setts were re-colonised almost immediately. A considerable amount of re-gassing was therefore necessary. Between November 1975 and May 1980 107 badgers and 100 faeces samples were taken for laboratory examination; 14 of the badgers were found to be infected with bovine TB, but all the faeces samples proved negative.

The present situation in the Thornbury experimental area is that badger activity has been reduced to a low level, with most of the setts derelict and very little re-gassing necessary. No tuberculous badgers have been found in the area since March 1978, and since February 1978 repeated tuberculin testing of cattle in the area has revealed no reactors with visible TB lesions. MAFF plans to keep this area free of badgers and to continue to monitor the herds to see whether badger-clearance results in freedom from TB in the cattle.

3. Cornwall

The clearance operations in Cornwall have, on the whole, been on a smaller scale than in Dorset and at Thornbury. An analysis of the history of herds in certain parts of the county suggests that outbreaks of bovine TB follow a distinct pattern. They tend to occur in small clusters, with all the farms in a group becoming affected at the same time. In each case this implies a common source of infection. In some instances the source of infection has gone undetected, but in others it has been traced to infected badgers.

The Kea and Feock parishes, lying immediately to the south of Truro, had a very low level of infection in the eight years from 1962 to 1970; only six reactors with visible lesions were removed from the entire area during this period. In 1970/71 a cluster of ten infected farms was discovered, and over a 12 month period 50 reactors with visible lesions were removed. The outbreak was investigated by MAFF's veterinary officers, but the source of infection was not discovered.

Annual tests continued to be made on all the herds in the area, but no reactors with visible lesions were found until 1975/76, when two clusters of TB infection were identified, one involving five farms at the eastern end of the area, the other involving three farms at the western end. Infection continued in one of the farms in this latter group until June 1978. An infected badger was discovered on this farm in November 1977 and shortly after gassing of setts was started on the farm and in the areas adjacent to it. Since then only two reactors with visible lesions have been found (both in August 1978). These animals had probably been infected before gassing commenced.

The outbreak in the eastern part of Kea parish died down, but the origin of infection in this area was not detected. No visible-lesion reactors were found in 1977, but in 1978 a reactor in another area was traced back to a farm in this part of Kea. This farm had held a sale in February 1978 and a subsequent investigation of stock sold by the farmer in question revealed nine animals with visible tuberculous lesions. At the same time three reactors were removed from a neighbouring farm.

In May 1978 a badger carcase removed from this area was found on *post-mortem* examination to be infected with bovine TB. Authority to gas was granted, but since the badgers in this particular area had been the subject of a special study by MAFF scientists, it was decided to remove the badgers by trapping rather than gassing. Of the 29 badgers removed, ten were found at autopsy to be infected with the disease. In one social group all eight animals were found to be infected. Following this clearance operation, no further reactors have been found in the herds in the area.

A similar story can be told about the Polyphant area of North Cornwall. The herds in the immediate vicinity of the hamlet of Polyphant were free of infection in the 12 years from 1963 to 1975. Throughout the period however small clusters of outbreaks were occurring in neighbouring areas. Then between 1975 and 1979 a group of five farms near Polyphant became infected. One reactor with visible lesions was taken from each. A badger was caught in the area in April 1978, and was found to be infected with TB. Following a survey of badger setts, gassing commenced in December 1978. Since February 1979 no further visible-lesion reactors have been found.

4. Herd Translocation – Devon

At a meeting arranged by the Cornwall County Branch of the National Farmers' Union, one of the farmers present told me about one of his colleagues who suffered an outbreak of bovine TB soon after moving his entire, hitherto TB-free, herd from Yorkshire to Devon. This case was checked with MAFF, who were able to substantiate the story.

It appears that the farmer in question ran a Friesian milking herd in Yorkshire and that between 1962 and 1970 regular tuberculin tests had disclosed no reactors. The farmer moved to Devon in 1970 and took 41 cattle with him. He also purchased one animal from the previous occupier of the farm, the rest of the previous occupier's stock having been sold off. All the cattle, including the purchased animal, tested clear in April 1971. Before the next test the cow that had been bought was disposed of. A reactor was then recorded in 1975. This was an animal that had given an inconclusive response to the tuberculin test in December 1972 and in January 1973. More cattle started to react positively and were removed. Then TB appeared in neighbouring herds. After a thorough investigation of all these outbreaks, an infected badger was found in September 1977. By this time the farm in question and two adjoining farms were severely infected. An official badger survey was started in October 1977, and the whole area was subsequently gassed.

5. Lower Tresmorne Farm, Bude, Cornwall

This farm of about 150 acres is run by Mr C L Barrell who wrote to me on 15 November 1979 giving details of the problems he has had with bovine TB in his herd.

"I am a small tenant dairy farmer. I have been farming for 16 years, and after eight years I moved to this farm. Two years later I had tuberculosis in the cows and young stock. It was financially very bad as the valuations at the time were very depressed. I lost a total of 74 animals out of a total of around 150. When restrictions were lifted after one year, the values had more than doubled, so with the compensation money I was only able to replace 12 animals!

"After intensive investigations it was proved that the outbreak was caused by badgers. Three infected badgers were found dead on the farm or nearby. The Ministry of Agriculture took no action as they had a court case pending against them.

"So it was hardly surprising that with infected badgers on the farm we were only able to stay clear for about 2½ years.

"One and a half years ago we had another crippling outbreak (I am still under restrictions) and this time I have lost nearly 50 animals. We found a badger dying (later proved to be from tuberculosis) in a field with my stock grazing it! Three infected badgers were found in the vicinity this time as well. The Ministry of Agriculture moved painfully slowly, but after seven months they started gassing and I hope at last we will be able to go clear.

"When we moved we were delighted to find amongst the wildlife an abundance of badgers. My wife and I are keen on conservation and it gave us great pleasure to see badgers.

"We believe that the best and only future for badgers is to have healthy badgers. It must be wrong to leave them infected and suffering over a long period, infecting others, as well as cattle, in a wider and wider area.

"The cattle are slaughtered at the very onset of the infection, while infected badgers are allowed to die in great pain, coughing and spitting infection in every direction.

74

"The one fact that I am certain of is that badgers will always re-inhabit gassed or empty setts. It must be in the conservationists' and the farmers' and taxpayers' best interest to destroy infected badgers as speedily as possible."

6. Raftra and Ardensawah Farms, St Levan, Cornwall

These farms are run by Mr J Hocking, who attended the meeting organised by the Cornwall County Branch of the NFU. In the course of this meeting, Mr Hocking gave details of his experience of TB in cattle and badger's on the two farms. His notes, reproduced below, and Tables 8 and 9 in Appendix I, summarise the case.

"The history of our tuberculin testing started in 1951 with a private test at Ardensawah carried out on 123 animals, of which 100 failed the test. The 23 that passed were removed to Raftra Farm. From that date, Raftra was carried on as a tuberculin-free herd, but there were continuous breakdowns (Table 8).

"At Ardensawah we did not test between 1951 and 1958. We carried on farming leaving all the reactors on the farm during that period. When the eradication programme started in 1958 we tested 123 animals at Ardensawah with the reverse results; 100 passing and 23 reactors. We had continuous minor breakdowns up till 1968 despite carrying out at tremendous expense, all the improvements recommended by Ministry of Agriculture officials. Between 1968 and 1973 we lost 84 head of cattle.

"In November 1972 we started to catch some badgers for the Ministry for post-mortem tests (Table 9). After the removal of the badgers the improvement in our testing results was unbelievable. Not only our farm, but the whole parish had clear tests for the first time since testing started.

"Controlling the number of badgers has become very controversial, but in our opinion it is a great necessity and best carried out by Ministry employees. We feel it would be very unpopular if the services of the Ministry were withdrawn as it could lead to the farming community taking the law into its own hands."

7. Oakford Farm, Chippenham, Wiltshire

The owner of this farm, Mr R Earle, wrote to me on 18 April 1980.

"I have farmed 197 acres of land near St Catherine's valley, Batheaston for the last 16 years and until now have had no trouble with TB.

"In December 1979 I found three dead badgers, two were too badly decayed to be of any use to the Ministry of Agriculture, but one was quite fresh and so I sent it to them for testing. Since then I have found another dead badger which I also sent off. All three badgers were found in the same area and were found after examination to have suffered from tuberculosis.

"On 11 January 1980 I had a routine tuberculin test on my cattle at which five reacted and three of these were found with visible lesions. These were the first reactors I have suffered in 20 years farming.

"On 18 March this year I had another test and this time I had nine reactors and two borderlines. It was thought unlikely that any of these would have visible lesions and that I might get a licence enabling me to buy in more cattle. However, it appears that seven of the animals had visible lesions.

"It seems certain that my cattle contracted tuberculosis from these badgers from the setts near where I found the badger carcases. The Ministry have last week gassed these setts approximately 3½ months from the time I sent the first dead badger to them.

"I believe that the problem started with the first Ministry gassing operations on my land. There was tuberculosis in a neighbour's cattle and so the Ministry gassed all the badger setts on my land even though my cattle were entirely free of the disease. At that time I had literally hundreds of badgers on the farm and I believe that all the diseased badgers were being kept off my farm by natural territorial methods. When the first gassing was completed the empty setts provided a perfect habitat for diseased badgers from other areas to move into. Possibly old badgers rejected by their own setts.

"This theory is substantiated by the fact that some of the badger runs change direction following gassing. Badger colonies became disorientated, split up and spread, carrying disease with them which subsequently spread to the cattle which had hitherto been free of it. Three farms, to my knowledge, are involved in this fresh outbreak, all of which have been free of tuberculosis for many years.

"I have asked the Ministry to take action against setts that we know to be infected but to leave those setts where there is no sign of tuberculosis and to use natural boundary, i.e. a brook, rather than the boundaries of the farm. It seems to me we need to build up a natural immunity where possible.

"At the time of writing I have been served with a compulsory gassing order allowing gassing over the whole 197 acres of my farm. This means that setts over half a mile from the source of the infection can be gassed, even though they almost certainly contain healthy badgers, but setts only 50 yards from the source of the infection cannot be gassed even though they almost certainly contain diseased badgers.

"It is unfortunate that the boundary of my farm, which is also the boundary of the original gassing area, runs straight through a small cluster of infected badger setts. The Ministry refused to gas these setts because they were outside the original gassing area."

8. Collery Farm, Kilkhampton Cornwall

Mr C Gardner, who farms 320 acres, wrote on 16 November 1979. His letter gives some idea of the financial losses that result from an outbreak of bovine TB.

"For the past 20 months we have had tuberculosis reactors on this farm, and so far there is little prospect of the situation improving. We are due for yet another test in a few weeks time, and have little hope of the results being negative.

"We keep a herd of good quality pedigree Friesian cows, and in addition to selling milk we rely in part on selling in-calf or newly calved pedigree heifers. We rear male calves and sell them as large steers in the spring when prices are at their highest for other farmers to fatten on grass during the summer.

"The history of our problem is as follows:

i.   No cattle have been brought into the farm for over six years, so we are confident the infection was not bought in.

ii.   On 20 March 1978 we had our annual test and all animals passed it.

iii. Only six weeks later we sent seven old cows for slaughter and the slaughterhouse inspector found one was infected.

iv.   As a result we had to re-test, on 10 July 1978, and five reactors went for slaughter.

v.   At re-test on 2 October 1978 one "dangerous contact" was slaughtered and 13 doubtfuls required re-testing.

vi.   On re-test, on 11 December 1978, they were passed as clear.

vii. On 5 February 1979 a test revealed one "dangerous contact" which was slaughtered.

viii. On 14 May 1979, 12 reactors were sent for slaughter, and many of these showed visible lesions.

ix.   On 24 September 1979 three reactors were sent for slaughter.

x.   A further test is due at the end of November or early December.

"Losses to the farm business can be summarised as follows:

i.   Fall in value of the animals since compensation for reactors is only three-quarters of value with a limit of £425. Many of our cows are worth £700-£800. Taking an average drop of £200 per animal (difference between true market value and compensation) the loss on 20 animals is £4000.

ii.   Loss of potential milk for four cows slaughtered in or near lactation, until this cow replaced by a heifer calving down: say ½ a lactation (herd average is 1,200 gallons per cow) 4 x 600 gallons = 2,400 gallons at 50p = £1.200.

iii. Drop in daily milk yield due to disturbance of cows at each test: 10 gallons each day of each test (6 x 2 x 10 gallons) = 120 gallons of milk at 50p = £60.

iv.   Loss of sale value of pedigree heifers which had to be kept to replace cows slaughtered for tuberculosis: 10 heifers at £550-£600 each = £5,750.

v.   Calving indexes became poor this year. Many have not held to AI the first time, and several that were in-calf have aborted for no apparent reason (vets confirm no infection). This means a loss of milk and a change in the herd management. Cows that do not calve regularly once a year have to be fed 13 and 14 months for 12 months output, thus eliminating the profit element. Difficult to put a figure on this.

vi.   Cost of repeated test. Each test involves two days, the first using four men for 3½ hours, and the second using four men for 2½ hours. This is 24 man hours per test. So far 6 tests = 6 x 24 = 144 hours at an average pay of £1.75 per hour: cost = £252.

vii.   Disruption to other work on the farm through taking labour to do tests cannot be costed.

viii.   Being unable to sell surplus heifers and male animals as forward stores in spring has meant more stock has had to be kept. This entails additional fertiliser to grow extra grass for them and has resulted in much corn being fed to fattening beef animals, while these animals would normally have been sold last spring at the peak of the market prices and the corn would have been available for sale at nearly £100 a ton. These animals have needed extra housing and labour, which have caused problems on the farm. A price cannot be given for this paragraph, but it could run into four figures.

ix.   The drop in the milk cheque, the drop in heifer sales, and the delay in selling beef animals, not to mention reduced revenue from sale of corn, has had a very bad effect on the cash-flow, causing difficulties at the bank.

"The total actual costs above amount to £11,262, more than a year's profit on many farms of this size. Taking into account reduced profit on selling beef animals less profitably, and loss of grain sales, the figure could well be £15,000 on this average size farm. It will take several years of trading to re-coup this loss and we have not yet seen the end of the matter.

"We know that our neighbour to the south found a badger which the Ministry of Agriculture confirmed was infected with tuberculosis in March 1979. We also know that the farms bordering us to the north have had tuberculosis problems and that infected badgers have been caught. Badgers travel several miles in a night and cross several farms and woods in that time. We know of no other source of the infection.

"We therefore urge you to look at this matter favourably and also to point out that we do not think any conservationist wishes to see badgers die of tuberculosis. To eradicate the disease will serve them as well as the farmers. Our cows must die to eradicate the infection and they do not seem to object to this."

APPENDIX IV

Procedure followed by MAFF after the disclosure of a Tuberculin Test Reactor

Routine tuberculin testing of cattle is generally carried out by local veterinary surgeons, with MAFF officers becoming involved only when a reactor or inconclusive reactor is found. If *post-mortem* examination of a reactor reveals visible lesions of TB, MAFF carries out an exhaustive investigation to try and find the origin of infection. A typical inquiry covers the following points:

The Reactor

1. The animal's history is traced, with particular attention paid to its origin (home-bred or purchased), any veterinary treatment, and whether it was alive at the time of any previous outbreaks of TB on the farm.

2. The animal's movements on the farm since the last tuberculin test are checked.

3. Where there are a number of reactors, whether they were at any time in the same group.

Other Animals

4. The farm's TB history is examined.

5. The history of TB in cattle on contiguous premises is checked.

6. The standard of fencing is inspected and the farmer is asked to provide details of any incidents of cattle straying onto or off his land.

7. Whether manure, nightsoil or similar fertilisers have been brought onto the farm; whether there has been access to slaughterhouse or knackeryard waste, including products used for feeding dogs; and whether raw milk, milk products or churn washings have been brought onto the farm and could have come into contact with stock.

8. The possibility of the disease having been introduced by a recent purchase is investigated.

9. Recent sales and deaths of cattle are investigated, including any animals that have been consigned to a knackeryard.

10. Whether cattle from other herds have been on the premises – for instance, whether a hired bull has been used and whether there are any rights of way through the farm for cattle from neighbouring premises.

11. Any goats on the premises are tuberculin tested.

12. Inquiries are made about the history of disease in other species of animal on the farm, especially pigs, cats and dogs.

Humans

13. Whether the farm adjoins a lay-by, caravan site or refuse tip.

14. The possibility that sewage or cesspool effluent might have contaminated pasture or drinking water is considered.

15. The farmer is asked whether he, his family, his employees or relief milkers have had any history of illness.

Other Sources

16. Recent use of, or alterations to, old buildings likely to have been contaminated in the past is checked.

17. The location of any nearby slaughterhouses or knackeryards is noted.

Where young stock are infected, inquiries are made about where they were reared. If this was not on the home farm but on a farm in different ownership or on temporary grazing, then the whole investigation is repeated for the farms concerned.

If this investigation fails to reveal the source of infection, the possibility that infected badgers might be involved is considered. MAFF's Divisional Veterinary Officer (DVO) asks the Divisional Executive Officer (DEO) to arrange for the collection of a sample of badgers and badger faeces for laboratory examination. The responsibility for carrying out this work lies with MAFF's Regional Pests Officer (RPO) who authorises his staff to carry out their investigation after having first consulted the Nature Conservancy Council to establish whether there are any nature reserves in the area to be surveyed. Wardens of nature reserves are given seven days notice of the start of the exercise.

The team responsible to the RPO maps the farm boundaries in the area under investigation and, if the farmers themselves are unable to supply badger carcases, the team searches for any freshly-dead badgers. Usually, however, it is necessary to catch the required specimens. In this case, the team looks for at least nine setts within a 1 to 2 kilometre radius of where the reactor was grazing, and collects at least five badgers, either by shooting or trapping, from different setts. In addition, faeces samples are taken from the badger latrines. This material is sent to the nearest MAFF Veterinary Investigation Centre where *post-mortem* examination of the badgers is carried out, and attempts are made to culture the tubercle bacillus.

If the results of the laboratory examination are negative, the investigation is carried no further unless reactors continue to be found, in which case another sample of badgers might be collected. If, on the other hand, any of the badgers in the sample are found to be infected with bovine tuberculosis, a full survey of the area in question is conducted. This is again done by the RPO's staff, who map all setts, latrines and badger tracks over an area of 9 square kilometres. Where the infected badgers are within one of the Control Areas defined in the Badgers (Control Areas) Order 1977, this detailed information is used by the DVO, DEO and RPO when they meet to decide the extent of the gassing operation. Having

80

settled this, the DEO notifies the Water Authority and the Local Authority and, subject to any comments they might have on the control operation, authorisation to commence gassing is granted.

Where the infected badgers are outside a Control Area, gassing may not start without reference to MAFF headquarters who are responsible for obtaining the views of the Consultative Panel whenever time allows and in any case where the investigation has taken place outside the South West.

APPENDIX V

Organisations represented on the Consultative Panel on Badgers and Tuberculosis

Agricultural Research Council
British Veterinary Association
Fauna Preservation Society
Country Landowners' Association
Mammal Society
National Farmers' Union
National Union of Agricultural and Allied Workers
Nature Conservancy Council
Royal Society for the Prevention of Cruelty to Animals
Society for Promotion of Nature Conservation
Universities Federation for Animal Welfare

APPENDIX VI

TB in Captive Animals

Introduction

In an account of TB in man and other animals published by the Medical Research Council in 1930, Dr H H Scott, then Pathologist to the Zoological Society of London, recorded that while tuberculous lesions in captive wild animals resembled those found in domesticated animals, there were three characteristic differences. First, not having been previously exposed to infection, captive animals had a low resistance to the disease which consequently ran a more rapid course. Second, dissemination generally took place early so that in spite of a short period of illness the animals were often found at autopsy to have widespread and advanced lesions. Third, up to the moment of death such animals often gave the appearance of being in excellent bodily condition.

Dr Scott pointed out that before 1925 the statistics of TB at the Zoological Gardens in Regents Park were insufficiently reliable to be used to illustrate the prevalence of the disease in captive animals. The inclusion in the figures of animals which contracted the disease before their arrival and which died soon after admission, together with the lack of any segregation for new arrivals, gave a false impression of the extent of TB at the Zoo.

In his report, Dr Scott recorded the detailed findings of *post-mortem* examinations of 70 cases of TB in mammals at the Zoo between January 1925 and July 1927. Only one case of bovine TB (in an Indian fruit bat) is recorded. More recent figures illustrating the incidence of the disease at Regents Park and Whipsnade Park are set out below.

Regents Park

The Pathologist's report on deaths in the Zoological Society's Gardens during 1930 records that 12 mammals, 26 birds and four reptiles died from TB that year, with bovine TB given as the cause of death in five of the mammals (a blackbuck, a sable antelope, a tiger, a sun bear, and an Indian fruit bat).

In 1935, the Society's Pathologist reported that the disease caused the deaths of seven mammals, 16 birds, five reptiles and one fish. The bovine tubercle bacillus was isolated in only one case, that of a female bushbuck.

The number of cases of TB at Regents Park between 1966 and 1978 is summarised in the following table:

	Total number of post-mortems	Number of specimens found to have TB
Mammals	4,876	10
Birds	5,083	65
Reptiles	1,832	25
Amphibia	433	8

Of the ten mammals examined, *M. bovis* was isolated in only one case, a recently-imported Rhesus monkey received in 1968 at the Institute of Comparative Medicine.

Whipsnade Park

There is little information about TB during the first 30 years of the Park's history, as a serious fire in the early 1960s destroyed most of the Park's early records.

In 1962, bovine TB was diagnosed in herds of Eland and Ankoli cattle sharing the same paddock in the centre of the Park. Between 1962 and 1966, 14 Eland and seven cattle were slaughtered following a positive reaction to the tuberculin test. Most of these animals were found to have typical lesions of TB and *M. bovis* was isolated in culture from about half the cases. Since 1966, further tuberculin tests have been negative, and *post-mortem* examinations have revealed no signs of the disease.

M bovis was also isolated from lesions in a Caracal lynx in 1963. It is not known whether there was any connection between this animal and the outbreak in the ruminants.

In 1964, lesions suggestive of TB were found in an Axis deer, and similar cases were found in subsequent years. Between 1970 and 1973 newborn animals were removed from the herd for hand rearing in the hope of establishing an uninfected herd. The adults were slaughtered over a period of two years.

Of the 46 Axis deer over three months of age examined during the period 1964/74, 23 had lesions suggestive of TB. Although one case each of *M bovis, M. avium* and *M. tuberculosis* was identified, most attempts to grow the organism in culture were unsuccessful. It was thought, therefore, that the cause of this infection was probably an atypical mycobactin-dependent mycobacterium of the sort which has frequently been isolated from deer, both in captivity and in the wild.

General

Amongst captive mammals throughout the world, bovine TB has been reported most frequently in ruminants, with large carnivores and primates figuring significantly amongst the other mammals affected. It is likely that captive mammals pick up the infection initially from ruminants and it would seem that most captive ruminants become infected from other related species. The original infection in many collections can probably be traced to domestic cattle in East Africa and South Asia, where in some areas bovine TB remains a considerable problem.

APPENDIX VII

The role of other animals in the epidemiology of TB of the Badger

J. Gallagher – Veterinary Investigation Centre, Elmbridge Court, Gloucester

Introduction

Two fundamental questions require an answer when considering the epidemiology of badger tuberculosis.

Firstly, is the badger currently being infected by another species, and secondly which animals are being infected by badgers?

Both questions can be answered largely by detailed examination of these species *post-mortem,* noting details about the disposition of all infected animals in relation to infected badgers, and also by an assessment of the stage of advancement or severity of disease in relation to the infected badgers in that area. Domesticated and free-living animals sharing the same habitat as the badger must both be considered.

Since all the cattle in South Gloucestershire and North Avon are still subject to annual tuberculin tests, there are detailed records of numbers of infected tuberculin reactors, their disposition and the stage of disease found in them. These have been studied in great depth by R H Muirhead, and considerable information is contained in a series of internal reports. A summary of the main findings is contained in the publication by Muirhead and others (1974). The information in this paper relates to the finding of tuberculosis in badgers in association with outbreaks of tuberculosis in cattle during a two-year period from April 1971 to April 1973. More information is now available with greatly increased numbers of badgers examined, and these findings are in close accord with the earlier results. During 1971-1973 in 60 per cent of herds where tuberculosis was diagnosed, infected badgers, or badger faeces, were found either on the farm or within half-a-mile of its boundaries. By 1975 this association was found in 75 per cent of herds (Muirhead and Gallagher 1976) and during 1977 evidence of badger infection was found in association with 90 per cent of herds.

During this six-and-a-half year period from 1971-1977 there were 21 infected animals showing 'open' lesions out of a total of over 1,000 cattle with tuberculosis. Only animals with gross visceral lesions were classed as 'open' cases, and those merely showing involvement of the lymph nodes at a likely portal of entry, for example only the lung nodes, were not considered 'open'.

Many of the pastures on the Cotswold hills are shared habitats of cattle and badgers. Setts are commonly found in woodland adjacent to pasture and both badger tracks and foraging areas may be seen with relative frequency on pasture land. Occasionally some quite large setts are found in fields. Local reports indicate that badgers may encroach deeply into the cattle habitat and invade cattle buildings in search of food. Both the general proximity of cattle and badgers and the opportunity for the spread of infection from one to another were readily apparent.

Sheep, as well as goats, are reputed to be moderately resistant to bovine strain tuberculosis, (Francis 1958). Routine slaughterhouse inspection of sheep from this area failed to show any evidence of tuberculosis during this six-and-a-half year period, nor indeed for many years previously. Even in the 'thirties' when tuberculosis was prevalent in cattle, sheep rarely became infected. For example, in America during 1938 only 18 cases of tuberculosis were found in 17,676,408 carcases examined. Typing was carried out in 17 cases and 14 yielded *M. avium*, (Report 1938). In the rare cases of tuberculosis recorded in sheep in Britain (McFadyean 1900, 1902, Griffiths 1925, Jowett 1928, Murphy 1935, Craig and Davies 1938 and Lovell and White 1941) amounting to a total of ten animals, eight were infected with *M. bovis* and two with *M. avium*. No further record of *M. bovis* infection in sheep in Britain has been found.

Horses are considered to be very resistant to bovine strain tuberculosis. (Innes 1949, Luke 1958). Only one case of tuberculosis was reported during this period of study and this was found to be due to *M. avium*. Advanced lesions involving the spleen, mesenteric nodes, liver and lungs, were observed in this animal. It had been grazing on pasture adjacent to a wildfowl park in which there was a considerable problem of tuberculosis in wild ducks.

Pigs, by contrast, are fairly susceptible to tuberculosis of the bovine, human and avian strains (Thornton 1949). Anthony (1940) reported an overall incidence of tuberculosis of 11 per cent out of 1,452,779 slaughter pigs examined in England. Rare cases of human strain infections have resulted from insanitary disposal of human excreta and from swill feeding. In an instance of the latter 30 per cent of 86 pigs fed swill from a tuberculosis sanitorium developed tuberculosis (Butler and Marsh 1927). During the present study period no bovine strain infection was reported from the local slaughterhouses and only two incidents of *M. avium* infection were disclosed. These two incidents involved pigs at pasture, and pigeons in a nearby wood were thought to be the origin of one of the cases. Only a very small number of pigs are kept at grass in this area, the great majority being housed (Report 1976).

The prevalence of bovine tuberculosis in dogs and cats dropped enormously during the latter part of the Cattle Tuberculosis Eradication Scheme (Lauder 1961). No *M. bovis* infections have been reported in these species either during this six-and-a-half year period or indeed for many years previously in this area. Local practices were asked to inform the VI Centre of possible cases of tuberculosis in dogs and cats and in January 1978 a single case of "mycobacterial bronchitis" was referred to the Centre. The subject was a three year-old beagle from the Thornbury area of Gloucestershire where many tuberculous badgers have been found. However, typing of the isolate involved showed it to be *M. fortuitum* which appeared to be causing a saprophytic colonisation of the exudates in the main airways, produced by a longstanding suppurative bronchopneumonia. The cause of initial pneumonia was not found due to prolonged antibiotic therapy.

Where severe outbreaks of tuberculosis were seen in several cattle herds in Pennsylvania in the United States during 1966-1968, four of nine dogs and 24 of 52 cats living on the farms were found to have tuberculosis (Snider, Cohen, Reif, Stein and Prier 1971). However, in contrast with the Gloucestershire situation, these animals lived exclusively in the cattle buildings and were subject to considerable challenge from the many cattle found showing discharging lesions, mostly in the lungs.

In the Gloucestershire area wildlife thus remain the only animals in which the existence of tuberculosis requires elucidation.

Materials and methods

Sampling was carried out in two areas where badger tuberculosis was known to exist – the Thornbury area of north Avon – and selected sites on the Cotswold hills. Cages were used for trapping, some of which had been specially designed by the Pests Department staff.

Post-mortem examination was carried out on all animals. Smears from suspect lesions were examined by Ziehl-Neelsen stain. In the larger species a collection of retropharyngeal, or pharyngeal, bronchial, mediastinal and mesenteric nodes was routinely taken for mycobacterial culture attempts. Lung,

Table 1: Wildlife collected from specified sites in Gloucestershire and Avon and examined at MAFF's Gloucester Veterinary Investigation Centre, 1973-76 (a)

	No. Examined No. M. bovis	No. Thornbury area	No. Cotswold Hills
Badgers *(Meles meles)*	498/118	98/11	400/107
Fox *(Vulpes vulpes)*	103/4	23/0 (2)*	80/4 (4)*
Woodmouse *(Apodemus sylvaticus)*	406/0	255/0 (4)*	151/0
Housemouse *(mus musculus)*	32/0	32/0	
Vole *(Microtus agrestis and Clethrionomys glareolus)*	507/0	437/0 (1)*	70/0
Shrew *(Sorex araneus)*	14/0	14/0	–
Rat *(Rattus norvegicus)*	85/0	83/0	2/0
Mole *(Talpa europaeus)*	20/0	16/0	4/0
Hedgehog *(Erinaceus europaeus)*	5/0	3/0	2/0
Rabbit *(Oryctolagus cuniculus)*	21/0	16/0	5/0
Weasel *(Mustela nivalis)*	10/0	6/0	4/0
Stoat *(Mustela erminea)*	1/0	1/0	–
Mink *(Mustela vison)*	2/0	–	2/0
Polecat ferret	1/0	–	1/0
Squirrel *(Sciurus carolinensis)*	36/0	17/0	19/0
Hare *(Lepus capensis)*	1/0	–	1/0
Cat *(Felis domesticus)*	2/0	2/0	–

Total examined — 1,742

Note: (a) All these animals are also recorded in Appendix 1, Table 12
( )* Isolations of other mycobacteria.

Table 2: Main mammalian species sharing the badger's habitat

Domesticated species

cattle	goats
pigs	horses
sheep	(deer)

Sett co-habitants or inhabitants of vacant setts*

foxes	feral and wild cats
rabbits	polecat
rats	polecat ferret
bank vole	weasel
woodmouse	

Prey species*

rabbits (young)	shrews
hares (young)	moles
rats (young)	squirrels (carrion)
hedgehogs (young)	lambs (carrion)
voles	deer (carrion)
mice	

* After Neal (1977).

Table 3: Results of examination of badgers and foxes trapped on two farms where foxes were found infected with TB.

	Farm A		Farm B	
	Badgers	Foxes	Badgers	Foxes
No. animals examined	35	4	13	3
No. infected *M. bovis*	12†	2	3*	2
No. showing gross lesions of tuberculosis	8	Nil	Nil	Nil

* Three of seven badger faeces collected October 1973 were infected with *M. Bovis*
† One case of *M. avium* infection also found.

liver and spleen were taken from small rodents and usually sets of viscera were pooled in lots of two or three for culture. Isolation was attempted by culture only, using the techniques previously described (Gallagher and Horwill 1977) except that cultures were maintained for eight weeks before being discarded.

Results

A total of 1,244 animals belonging to 15 separate wildlife species was examined. Two stray cats were also examined. No distinction was made between field and bank voles, both species being grouped together as 'voles'. Of these animals most were obtained from the Thornbury area, where a particularly intensive trapping effort was made. The numbers of different species examined and the result of mycobacterial isolation attempts are shown in Table 1. The ecological relationship to the badger of the separate wildlife and domestic species is shown in Table 2. *M. bovis* was isolated from only four foxes, none of which showed macroscopic lesions at autopsy. These four animals were trapped at two separate locations on the Cotswold hills where severe cases of tuberculosis in badgers had been found (Table 3).

At one location eight out of 36 badgers examined showed gross lesions of tuberculosis at autopsy, three of which showed tuberculous pneumonia accompanied by tuberculous nephritis in one case. Of the remaining badgers showing no macroscopic lesions four were found to have latent *M. bovis* infections.

At the other location, no badgers showing gross lesions of tuberculosis were found but three of the 13 examined were infected with *M. bovis*.

M. avium was isolated from six foxes but no gross lesions were observed at autopsy.

Unidentified mycobacteria, not pathogenic to guinea pigs and causing no tuberculin sensitisation in them, were isolated from four woodmice and one vole. Due to heavy contaminant growths and poor vitality, these isolates could not be recovered in pure culture for typing.

Discussion

The other mammal species which the badger may encounter can conveniently be divided into domestic animals which might share foraging areas, species which might become residents of badger setts and species on which the badger preys.

Considering the last category, mammals are undoubtedly an important source of food for the badger. They may constitute from 10 to 30 per cent of the total diet although they may be completely absent from the diet for some parts of the year (Barker 1969). The badger with its short stout legs and heavy body, is not physically suited to capture adult large mammals but it does prey on the very young nestlings (Neal 1977). The majority of these species, such as rabbits, hares and hedgehogs, have their young in the Spring and Summer and it is at these times that most of the mammal prey species are eaten.

The commonest rodent eaten is the field vole *(Microtus agrestis)* and even when the bank vole *(Clethrionomys glareolus)* is abundant the former appears to be preferred, or possibly more easily caught (Neal 1977).

Wells (1937 and 1946) examined 4,309 field voles from 1936 to 1939 and found 20 per cent infected with *M. microti*. Although tuberculosis was widespread in cattle at that time, no isolations of *M. bovis* were made. The sampling areas were in Wales, South England and Oxfordshire. Many affected animals showed subcutaneous caseous granules and occasionally lesions in the lungs and elsewhere. Infection rates varied from 0 to 66 per cent in different areas and at different times in the same area. A considerable variation was found even between contiguous groups, probably as a result of the very limited ranging activity of these animals. Brown (1956) estimated the home range to be 975m^2 with most animals moving less than 27m.

Wells (1946) considered that infection was spread by the ingestion of excreta and cadavers of diseased voles and also by bite wounding during fighting.

223 bank voles were also examined by Wells and 10.3 per cent were infected with *M. microti*. Shrews and woodmice were examined but this infection was observed infrequently (1.4 per cent infected of 550 examined and 2.3 per cent of 175 examined respectively). There are no records of *M. microti* infection in wildlife since the early 1940s and its persistence in small rodents until present times is debatable. In a survey of the prevalence of this infection in small rodents Little (pers comm.) failed to find any infected animals. Indeed, it would be surprising if this disease maintained over a long period in these populations since their lifespans are so brief. The lifespan of bank voles has been estimated as on average 2.2 to 3.2 months (Bobek 1969), field voles 7.5 months (Leslie and Rawson 1940), woodmice 2 to 3.5 months (Flowerdew 1972), and shrews, the longest lived, 12 months (Michielson 1966).

The only small rodents from which mycobacteria were isolated during the investigation under report were one vole and four woodmice. Unfortunately these isolates could not be typed due to contamination and poor vitality but they did not show any characteristics of mammalian strains.

Laboratory mice have been found to be susceptible to both mammalian and avian mycobacteria by both the oral and respiratory routes although large doses were used (Pierce, Dubos and Middlebrook 1947, Glover 1944). Schalk *et al* (1935) showed that wild field mice and common mice were highly resistant to avian tuberculosis. Although fed cultures and minced tissues from tuberculous fowls, none of 74 mice used showed any lesions of tuberculosis at autopsy.

Few rabbits were trapped for autopsy, largely as a result of a series of epidemics of myxomatosis which had completely destroyed the rabbit population in many areas. However, no authenticated cases of spontaneous tuberculosis have been reported in wild rabbits, although, as Cobbett (1917) observed, rabbits must frequently have grazed pastures heavily infected by cattle and under such conditions domestic pigs readily became infected. Rabbits are highly susceptible to tuberculosis, 30 bovine type bacilli being sufficient to produce severe generalised disease following experimental infection by inhalation (Lurie, Happleston, Abramson and Swartz 1950). If infection had been picked up by wild rabbits it seems likely that it would have spread amongst them whilst in the confines of their burrows. Lurie (1941) observed that aerogenous infection readily spreads from a group of experimentally-infected rabbits to clean rabbits segregated from them by a mesh barrier. 79 per cent of the 89 rabbits used showed clinical signs of tuberculosis from 4.8 to 6.5 months later.

Cobbett (1917) considered that the absence of tuberculosis in rabbits at a time when the disease was rife in cattle was due to their 'clean grazing' habits. "Rabbits have an extremely sensitive nose which allows them to avoid soiled grass." Hares were infrequently seen in the sample areas but in an intensive trapping exercise Matthew and Sargent (1977) examined 285 hares and found only *M. avium* in four cases.

Griffiths (1939) recorded a case of *M. bovis* infection in a hedgehog in Regents Park, London but it was thought to have been fed on infected cow's milk for some time. No further cases of this infection have been recorded in hedgehogs in Britain, but Matthew and McDiarmid (1977) isolated *M. avium* from one of five carcases examined.

Hedgehogs rarely feature in the badger's diet according to Bradbury (1974) although young and adult may be eaten. The latter are probably only eaten by certain badgers which have the necessary resources to both kill and "open" the carcase (Chapman 1977).

Moles may be eaten occasionally and two out of 59 examined at the Truro Veterinary Investigation Centre were found to be infected with *M. bovis* (Report 1976). However, no macroscopic lesions were observed and these animals were trapped in an area where open cases of tuberculosis in badgers had been found. Neal (1977) describes how badgers have been known to excavate mole runs and devour nests of young and it seems likely that such an invasion may have resulted in the spread of infection to the moles.

The sample of both moles and hedgehogs examined from the Gloucester area is small but neither species was abundant at the sampling sites.

The main prey species of the badger is the earthworm which is eaten in large quantities (Kruuk and Parish 1977) and which might be considered to have some role as a passive transport host. Feeding on, or around, carcases of infected badgers might result in its being host to tubercle bacilli for a short period. Schalk (1935) explored the possibility of transport infection experimentally using earth heavily seeded with *M. avium* into which he placed several hundred earthworms. There they remained for a couple of weeks, but when removed and fed on clean soil for only a few days he failed to recover any organisms.

From these findings it seems a remote possibility that the earthworm has any direct significance in the epidemiology of badger tuberculosis although a more tenuous connection is discussed later. Also, infection of badgers through the agency of mammalian prey species is most unlikely.

This conclusion is supported by the very infrequent finding of alimentary origin infection in badgers. Only one of the 149 infected badgers examined showed obvious gut entry infection and this was a cub thought to have milk-borne infection. Two further cases were found in adults in a series of 36 infected badgers examined (Gallagher *et al* 1976) making a total of 1.6 per cent gut infections.

Considering the next groups of mammals, ones which may take up residence in badger setts, the majority do so when the sett has been vacated by the badgers, or they inhabit a disused part of the sett. Infection is thus unlikely to be by contagion between these species and badgers but by indirect means, the most likely being fomites of infected saliva or faeces remaining on badger bedding, or by inhalation of contaminated dust. The four foxes with *M. bovis* infection might have become infected by these means. However, since they are carrion eaters it is possible that they might alternatively have eaten an infected badger carcase. At one of these two sites where the infected foxes had been trapped, three badgers were suffering a fairly advanced tuberculous pneumonia and it seems likely that some deaths due to tuberculosis had occurred. At the other site, although none of the infected badgers showed gross lesions, three of seven badger faeces samples collected in October 1973 from this site were infected with *M. bovis*. This finding implies the presence of a badger with tuberculous pneumonia which had probably died in the meantime.

Since macroscopic lesions were not found in these foxes, the likely portal of entry of infection could not be established, however the lack of gross lesions implies the absence of a significant portal of exit of infection so that at this stage of the disease onward transmission would be a remote possibility.

Whether the infection in the foxes would have been progressive is speculative. There appears to be no record of bovine tuberculosis in red foxes; the only cases recorded being in a mutant strain called the silver fox. According to Sterk (1940), affected silver foxes developed generalised disease, with tubercle formations in the lungs, kidneys and spleen. These foxes were bred on fur farms where they were often subject to massive infection from their diet of uncooked cattle flesh, at a time when cattle tuberculosis was rife. Primary lesions were only found in the intestine. Intestinal ulcers often developed and the mesenteric lymph nodes usually contained caseous abscesses. Whether the silver fox was genetically more susceptible to tuberculosis than the wild red fox is unknown. The canidiae appear to have some measure of native immunity to tuberculosis (Francis 1959), but no information was found on the likely susceptibility of the red fox. Clearly, the heavy challenge of infection presented to the silver foxes on fur farms would make generalised disease a likely outcome.

Badger lesions contain relatively far higher numbers of bacilli than those of cattle (Gallagher *et al* 1976) and should foxes eat badger tissues, infection may establish. However, it would appear that foxes generally fear the badger and are unlikely often to eat badger carcases. During feeding preference experiments. MacDonald (1977) found that the two foxes under experiment appeared to be frightened of a badger carcase he introduced to them, and they shied away from it. Subsequently they urine marked the carcase but made no attempt to eat it. However, some hungry fox in the countryside may well be tempted.

Rats are likely to devour virtually any carrion although they have a very high natural resistance to tuberculosis (Wessels 1941). Schalk (1935) demonstrated that they could act as mechanical carriers of avian tubercle bacilli. In a series of well ordered experiments he demonstrated that even when fed minced tuberculous organs of fowls containing very large numbers of organisms, the rats did not develop tuberculous lesions but their faeces were heavily infected. He showed that rats infesting a chicken pen containing tuberculous birds could act as transport hosts in this manner and spread infection both to clean birds and pigs housed on the same premises.

No evidence was found that the rat was acting as transport host in the spread of badger tuberculosis in the Gloucestershire area. However, whilst examining a selection of wildlife species in an area where a severe outbreak of badger tuberculosis had been found in Dorset, Little (pers comm) isolated *M. bovis* from three out of 95 rats examined. Badgers were dying of tuberculosis in this area and the rat population was high. None of the infected rats showed gross lesions and thus the route of infection was unknown. However, it is not unreasonable to suggest that these infections resulted from feeding on badger carrion. The rats might have acted as transport hosts but there was no evidence that they were other than secondary hosts of the badger disease.

A case of bovine strain tuberculosis in a fallow deer was found in the Irish Republic in an area where tuberculosis in cattle had persisted (Wilson and Harrington 1976). There are no records of *M. bovis* infection in deer in this country although they have been examined exhaustively; mycobacteria recovered have either been *M. avium* type A2 or a strain of *M. johneii* (Rankin and McDiarmid 1968, Anon 1973). A herd of deer is located in the Thornbury area but no specimens were available for examination. Inspection of carcases is carried out and no cases of tuberculosis have been reported.

In Gloucestershire cattle are the only domestic species in which tuberculosis due to *M. bovis* has been found. As previously mentioned, the number of infected animals was small and the proportion of these showing open lesions was very low: approximately 2 per cent. In the context of the total bovine population, the number of cattle excreting tubercle bacilli appears of no consequence in the maintenance of tuberculosis in badgers, and of very little consequence in its maintenance in cattle.

In contrast, the overall prevalence of tuberculosis in badgers has been approximately 20 per cent and half these showed open lesions, usually capable of shedding large numbers of tubercle bacilli. Since infected badger communities may contain from 20 per cent to c. 60 per cent of infected individuals (Gallagher 1980) and infection may be spread from one community to another during fighting as well as emigration, the transmission of tuberculosis in badgers seems completely independent of infection from other species.

The transmission of infection to cattle is likely to occur as a result of contamination of pasture or cattle feeds by infected badgers' sputum, urine, faeces or discharges from bite wounds. However, the lesions of tuberculosis in cattle were most frequently seen in the broncho-mediastinal lymph nodes and the retropharyngeal nodes. Occasionally the prescapular node alone was affected (Muirhead pers comm).

Retropharyngeal node involvement is consistent with either respiratory or alimentary route infection (Hutyra *et al* 1949) and since infection is likely to enter by ingestion, gut involvement might be expected. However, the absence of cases of gut involvement is not incompatible with this hypothesis. A large proportion of, and possibly all, eructated rumen gas passes through the lungs prior to being expelled (Waldo and Hoernicke 1966). Thus it is possible that aerosols of tubercle bacilli in the rumen gas may be transported to the lungs. Using non-pathogenic marker organisms Mullenax and others (1964) showed that in fact appreciable numbers of bacteria were conveyed to the lungs during eructation. This finding is highly pertinent to possible establishment of a tuberculosis infection in the lungs following ingestion of contaminated feed since the dose of tubercle bacilli required to establish infection via the lungs is considerably less than is required to establish infection of the gut (Sigurdsson 1945). This route of infection may occur in a number of infected cattle but inquisitive cattle may also inhale infected aerosols directly by sniffing badger excreta. Infection of the prescapular node is seen on very rare occasions and implies entry of the organism through the skin and this infection most probably occurs as a result of contamination of foot lesions.

The role of other animals in the epidemiology of badger tuberculosis may thus be postulated as shown in Figure 1.

Badgers are acting as a self-perpetuating reservoir of tuberculosis and overspill of infection may result in chance infection of other species. Foxes might act as a secondary reservoir of infection, although the evidence at the moment indicates that they are "blind end" hosts, as the cases encountered would be extremely unlikely to transmit the infection onwards. Rats might act as transport hosts although this is likely to be limited to the proximity of the original source of infection. Cattle, sheep, and deer are susceptible hosts, but the cattle, being the most susceptible and the most abundant in the infected badger areas, are the only domestic species in which infection has been found.

A further aspect pertinent to this conclusion is that badgers most prefer pasture land for foraging to the remainder of their habitat (Kruuk and Parish 1977). Permanent pasture is preferred to rotational grazing (Kruuk, Parish, Brown and Carrera 1979) and the former is more prevalent on the slopes of the Cotswold hills where it is predominantly used for cattle grazing. The abundance of the earthworm, *Lumbricus terrestris,* has been found to be the major determining factor in this preference and indeed the biomass of this worm appears one of the important determinants in badger population size (Kruuk and Parish 1977, Kruuk 1978).

The frequency of *M. avium* infection in foxes deserves some comment. Six per cent of all foxes yielded these organisms from their lymph nodes although no macroscopical lesions were found. *M. avium* infection in foxes is, of course, not unexpected from the sometimes quite high bird-component of their diet (Corbett and Southern 1978). The strains involved have all been type A II.

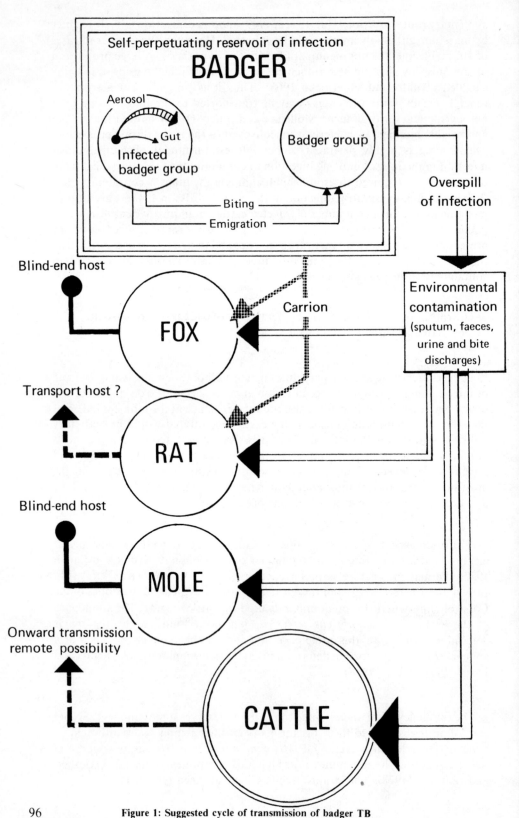

Figure 1: Suggested cycle of transmission of badger TB

References

Anon. (1973) Diseases of Deer, Members Information Supplement. *Vet. Rec* **92** No. 13.

Anthony, D.J. (1940) *Diseases of the Pig and Its Husbandry.* Bailliére, Tindall and Cox, London.

Barker, G.M.A. (1969) Wytham Badger Survey — Diet cit. Neal, E.G. *Badgers,* Blandford Press, Poole, Dorset.

Bobek, B. (1969) *Acta. Theriol.* **14** 191.

Bradbury, K (1974) The Badger's Diet in Paget, R.J. and Middleton, A.L.V, *Badgers of Yorkshire and Humberside,* Ebor, York.

Brown, L.E. (1956) *J. Anim. Ecol.* **25** 54.

Butler, W.J. and Marsh, H. (1927) *J. Amer. Vet. Med.* Assoc. **70** 786.

Chapman, J.F. (1977) cit. *Badgers,* Neal. E.G. Blandford Press, Poole, Dorset.

Cobbett, L. (1917) *The Causes of Tuberculosis,* p. 136 Cambridge Public Health Series, London. Cambridge Univ. Press.

Corbett, G.B. and Southern, H.N. (1978) *The Handbook of British Mammals 2nd edn.* Blackwell, Oxford.

Craig, J.F. and Davis, G.O. (1938) *Vet. Record* **43** 1156.

Flowerdew, J.R. (1972) *J. Anim. Ecol.* **41** 553.

Francis, J. (1958) *Tuberculosis in Animals and Man* Cassell & Co.,Ltd.,London.

Gallagher, J. (1980) Thesis, London Univ. in prep.

Gallagher, J. and Horwill, D.M. (1977) *J. Hyg., Camb.* **79** 155.

Gallagher, J., Muirhead, R.H. and Burn, K.J. (1976) *Vet. Record* **98** 9.

Glover, R. (1944) cit. Francis J. 1958 *Tuberculosis in Animals and Man,* Cassell & Co Ltd., London.

Griffiths, A.S. (1925) *Ibid.* **38** 157.

Griffiths, A.S. (1939) *Proc. Royal Soc. Medicine* **32** 1045.

Hutra, F., Marek, J. and Mamninger, R. (1949) *Special Pathology and Therapeutics of the Diseases of Domestic Animals* 5th edn. Bailliére, Tindall and Cox, London.

Innes, J.R.M. and Wilkins, J.H. (1949) *Brit. Vet. Jour.* **105** 282.

Jowett, W. (1928) *Ibid.* **41** 255.

Kruuk. H. (1978) *J. Zool. London* **184** 1.

Kruuk, H. and Parish, T. (1977) *Behaviour of Badgers* 1st. edn. pub. Institute of Terrestrial Ecology. Cambridge.

Kruuk, H., Parish, T., Brown, C.A.J. and Carrera, J. (1979) *Journal of Applied Ecology* **16** 453.

Lauder, I.M. (1961) *Tuberculosis in animals,* Symposia of the Zoological Society of London, No. 4 ed. J.N. Ritchie and W.D. Macrae. The Society 37.

Leslie, P.H. and Ranson, R.M. (1940) *J. Anim. Ecol.* **9** 27.

Lovell, R. and White, E.G. (1941) *Brit. Journ. Tuberc.* **35** 28.

Luke, D. (1958) *Vet. Record* **76** (26) 529.

Lurie, M.B. (1941) cit. Francis, J. 1958 *Tuberculosis in Animals and Man.* Cassell & Co., Ltd., London.

Lurie, M.B. Heppleston, A.G., Abramson, S. and Swartz, I.B. (1950) *Amee. Rev. Tuberc.* **61** 765.

MacDonald, D.W. (1977) *Mammal Review (No. 1)* **7** 7.

Matthews, P.R.J. and McDiarmid, A. (1977) *Res. vet. Sci.* **22** 388.

Matthews, P.R.J. and Sargent, A. (1977) *Brit, vet. J.* **133** 399.

McFadyean, J. (1900) *Jour. Comp. Path* **13** 59.

McFadyean, J. (1902) *Ibid.* **15** 158.

Michielsen (1966) cit. Corbett, G.B. and Southern, H.N. *The Handbook of British Mammals,* Blackwell, Oxford.

Muirhead, R.H. and Gallagher, J. (1976) *The Veterinary Annual* 16th issue 237.

Muirhead, R.H. Gallagher, J. and Burn, K.J. (1974) *Vet. Record* **95** (24) 552.

Mullenax, C.B., Allison, M.J. and Sanger, R. (1964) *Am. Jour. vet. Res.* **25** 1583.

Murphy, J.M. (1935) *Vet. Record* **40** 1488.

Neal, E.G. (1977) *Badgers,* Blandford Press, Poole, Dorset.

Pierce, D. Dubos, R.J. and Middlebrook, G. (1947) cit. Francis J. 1958 *Tuberculosis in Animals and Man.* Cassell and Co., Ltd., London.

Rankin, J.D. and McDiarmid, A. (1968) *Symp. zool. Soc.,* London, No 24 119.

Report (1938) *Bureau of Animal Industry USA:* Report of year ending June 30th 1938.

Report (1976) *Bovine Tuberculosis in Badgers,* MAFF, London.

Report (1976) *Gloucester VI Centre,* Annual Report.

Schalk, A.F., Roderick, Z.M., Foust, H.L. and Harshfield, G.S. (1935) *Avian Tuberculosis — collected studies* Agricultural Experiment Station, North Dakota Agricultural College, Fargo, North Dakota. Bull. 27.

Sigurdsson, J. (1945) *Acta. Tuberc. Scand.* Sup. 15.

Snider, W.R., Cohen, D., Reif, J.S., Stein, S.C. and Prier, J.E. (1971) *Am. Rev. Resp. Dis.* **104** 866.

Sterk. G. (1940) Vet. Bull. 1942 **12** 438 abstract from *Dtsch. Tieräzil Wschr.* **42** 382.

Thornton, H. (1949) *Textbook of Meat Inspection,* 4th. edn. Balliére, Tindall and Cox, London.

Waldo. D.R. and Hoernicke, H. (1966) *Jour. Dairy Sci.* **44** 1766.

Wells, A.Q. (1937) *Lancet* (1) 1221.

Wells, A.Q., Ratcliffe, H.L. and Crumb, C. (1948) *Amer. J. Hyg.* **47** 11.

Wessels, C.C. (1941) *Amer. Rev. Tuberc. pulm. Dis.* **43** 637.

Wilson, P. and Harrington, R. (1976) *Vet. Record.* **98** 74.

APPENDIX VIII

The ecology of the Badger

Background

Early in 1975 MAFF and the Nature Conservancy Council agreed that more information was needed about badger ecology to help understand the role of badgers in the transmission of TB to cattle. Accordingly, a research project was launched in Gloucestershire in the summer of 1975 under the auspices of the Land Pests and Birds Department of the Pest Infestation Control Laboratory, now part of the Agricultural Science Service of MAFF's Agricultural Development and Advisory Service (ADAS).

Location of Project

The site is situated in a deep valley in the Cotswold escarpment, and covers an area of some 9 square kms. in which there now live about 200 badgers divided into 28 social groups. Although predominantly woodland, the study area includes tenanted grazing land let to neighbouring farms, together with some summer grazings let annually under licence. The project has been supported by the local farmers who from the start have been kept informed about its objectives and progress. As noted later in this Appendix, some are now becoming increasingly concerned about the threat to their cattle from tuberculous badgers within the study area.

Research Objectives

Very broadly the objectives of the project, as defined at the outset, fall under five headings:

(i) **Movement** – the range of badger movement within areas where there are unexplained reactors to the tuberculin test and the factors determining this range.

(ii) **Interaction** – contact between badgers and cattle, and the factors determining this contact.

(iii) **Population** – the factors governing badger population density and the effects of the removal of badgers from one area on the movement of badgers in neighbouring areas.

(iv) **Behaviour** – abnormal behaviour patterns of diseased badgers.

(v) **Deterrents** – whether badgers can be prevented from re-occupying vacant setts.

Study Techniques

A variety of techniques has been used (a) to track badgers, (b) to plot the home-range boundaries of individuals and (c) to delineate the territorial boundaries of each social group. The most important of these researchers techniques has been radio tracking, using small radio transmitters attached to the badgers by means of a leather collar. Extensive use has also been made of bait-marking, a technique which involves the laying of bait containing indigestible coloured plastic markers. The recovery of these markers from the badgers' faeces indicates which latrines badgers from each sett have visited. By plotting the results on a map a picture of the territories of each social group is built up. Tagging, using plastic numbered ear tags, and marking, by applying tattoos with a hypographic machine, have also been employed, and have proved particularly useful in studying the dispersal of cubs and movements within the badger population.

Progress of the Research Programme

The movement of the badgers within the study area has been recorded in detail, and the sizes of their territories established. The range boundaries of social groups have remained relatively stable throughout the study period, the largest area covered by a group being 90 hectares and the smallest 15 hectares. Radio tracking has indicated that male badgers have larger home ranges than females (an average of 33.5 hectares compared with 12.6) and that individuals within a social group often display a marked preference for a particular area within the group's overall territory.

Radio tracking has also led to the understanding of the behaviour of badgers affected with bovine TB. It appears that it is not unusual for a sick badger to leave its social group and to live a solitary life in an outlying sett. Furthermore, tuberculous badgers have been found to transgress social group boundaries and, in one case, to seek refuge and food in a cow byre. The results of this work, which have been written up with a view to publication, suggest that in some situations the abnormal behaviour displayed by infected badgers might increase the chances of the disease being transmitted to nearby cattle.

Badger removal exercises have been carried out within the study area and also in Avon and in Cornwall. These have provided much information about (a) the incidence of TB in badger groups, (b) natality, (c) mortality, (d) population density and (e) recolonisation of cleared setts. In the study area itself, there have been three such exercises, the results of which are discussed below in relation to the incidence of TB in the herds of cattle which graze land in, or live adjacent to, the study area.

Bovine TB in the Study Area

There has long been bovine TB in this part of Gloucestershire and since 1976 there has been a number of outbreaks of the disease in the farms bordering the study area. An infected badger was found in the study area in 1976, and in May 1977 the first of the removals was carried out after TB had been confirmed in one of the social groups in the west of the area. Of the 13 badgers which were examined *post-mortem*, six were found to be infected with bovine TB. The second removal took place in August 1978 when, because of infection in two nearby herds of cattle, it was decided to remove by cage trapping six social groups at the eastern end of the study area, together with three groups on adjacent land. Of the 47 badgers caught, two revealed tuberculous lesions at autopsy. The third exercise was carried out in October and November 1979 following a herd break-down at the north eastern end of the study area. Five social groups were removed, and at least one member in four of the groups was found at autopsy to be infected. Of the 38 badgers removed, 12 were tuberculous.

Because of the importance of maintaining the co-operation of farmers in the area, payments additional to the usual rate of compensation were made by MAFF to those farmers who, on account of the research programme, experienced delays in the removal of the badgers associated with the outbreaks of TB in their cattle. This was done with the support of the Consultative Panel, which expressly recommended that the research programme should not be prematurely terminated.

Despite the increased level of compensation, it appears that support for MAFF's research programme varies amongst the farmers in the area, some of whom are worried about the threat to their cattle of cross-infection from the badgers. One wrote to me giving details of the difficulties that she and her husband were experiencing because of TB on their farm. After a TB-free record for almost 25 years, there was an outbreak of the disease in their herd in the autumn of 1977, when two cows were slaughtered as reactors. In November 1979 a freshly-calved heifer and in January 1980 a valuable Hereford bull had also to be slaughtered. This outbreak was associated with infection in the badgers in the study area and, because of the delay in removing the animals MAFF has made payments in addition to compensation. However, the complaint was made that they had not received "the same measure of protection against tuberculosis afforded by the Ministry to the rest of this country's farmers" and that "only one social group has been removed from our area since our first breakdown, and none since our second breakdown". The following additional points were made:

"1. If the Ministry of Agriculture wishes to carry out experimental work in the field of badger ecology which may endanger the health of cattle, it should provide its own Ministry farms on which to do it, and **not** put at risk the cattle and livelihood of private individuals.

2. If we are to be the hosts of this project we should be fully compensated financially in **all** respects and not subject to the Ministry's "upper limits".

3. If this project is to continue, we should know for how long. The strain of uncertainty is almost impossible to work under when it is one's livelihood at stake.

4. From the time of our first breakdown we have listened to the views of different factions of the Ministry and to the views of scientists and

conservationists – there seems to be little time for the view that this is our farm and not a laboratory."

Such feelings are by no means universal among the farmers whose cattle graze land in and around the study area. One farmer whom I met said that he was in favour of the project continuing despite the considerable financial losses he had suffered as a result of an outbreak of TB which MAFF found to be associated with infected badgers.

APPENDIX IX

Submissions and Acknowledgements

(a) **Organisations which submitted written evidence**

British Veterinary Association
Compassion in World Farming
Cornwall Badgers Protection League
Cornwall Naturalists Trust
Cotswold Wildlife Preservation Society
Crusade Against All Cruelty to Animals
Dartmoor Badgers Protection League
Devon Trust for Nature Conservation
Friends of the Earth
Mammal Society
Ministry of Agriculture, Fisheries & Food
National Farmers' Union (Cornwall and West Wiltshire County Branches)
National Society for the Abolition of Cruel Sports
Nature Conservancy Council
Royal Society for the Prevention of Cruelty to Animals
Society for the Promotion of Nature Conservation
Wiltshire Trust for Nature Conservation

(b) In addition letters and written submissions either for or against MAFF policy were received from 98 individuals including three Members of Parliament. Two petitions against MAFF policy that were supported by many signatures were also received.

(c) **Oral evidence provided by:**

(i) *Organisations*

Avon Wildlife Trust
Consultative Panel on Badgers and Tuberculosis (see Appendix V)
Cornwall Badgers Protection League
Cotswold Wildlife Preservation Society
Dartmoor Badgers Protection League
Devon Trust for Nature Conservation
Dorset Trust for Nature Conservation
Gloucester Trust for Nature Conservation
Wiltshire Trust for Nature Conservation

(ii) *Individuals*

Mr Axford (Uppacott Farm, Kilkhampton, Cornwall)
Mr Badcock (Beersheba Farm, St Ives, Cornwall)
Mr Barrell (Lower Tresmorne Farm, Bude, Cornwall)
Dr P Barrow (formerly London School of Hygiene and Tropical Medicine)
Mr I Beales (Deputy Editor, Western Daily Press)

Mr C Bone (Lanyan Farm, Penzance, Cornwall)
Dr B R Cook (Bayer UK Ltd)
Mr Curwen (Boundary Court Farm, Gloucestershire)
Mr B Hocking (Trengothal Farm, Penzance, Cornwall)
Dr H Kruuk (Institute of Terrestrial Ecology, Banchory)
Mr & Mrs Murray (Field Study Centre, Dartmoor)
Dr E Neal
Mr Richardson MRCVS (Cornwall Veterinary Association)

(d) In addition I should particularly like to thank Sir William Henderson, DSc, FRCVS, FRS, lately Secretary of the Agricultural Research Council; Dr L. G. Goodwin, CMG, FRCP, FRS, until recently Director of Science of the Zoological Society of London; Dr W. Plowright, CMG, DVSc, FRCVS, Head of the Department of Microbiology at the ARC's Institute for Research on Animal Diseases; and Professor R. Canivenc of the University of Bordeaux, for their advice on various epidemiological and biological aspects of my enquiry.

I am also grateful to Mr E. D. Clements for bringing up to date the Mammal Society figures for the distribution of badgers (Appendix II); to Dr B. R. Cook, lately of the New Zealand Ministry of Agriculture, for information about the opossum (paragraph 47); to Mr Gallagher, for providing the paper under his name in Appendix VII; and finally to Miss Eunice D. Overend, of the Wiltshire Trust for Nature Conservation, and to Mr Ian Beales, the Deputy Editor of the Western Daily Press, for focusing my attention, from opposite points of view, on the criticisms that have been made of your Department's policy.

APPENDIX X

References

Ahnlund, H. (1980). Sexual maturity and breeding season of the badger *(Meles meles)* in Sweden. *Journal of Zoology, London* **190**, 77-95.

Barcroft, J. (1931). The toxicity of atmospheres containing hydrocyanic acid gas. *Journal of Hygiene, Cambridge* **31** , 1-34.

Bell, P. (1976). Badgers and tuberculosis. *Country Life,* 1 July 1976.

Bouvier, G. (1963). Diseases of game and free-living animals in 1961/62 in Switzerland. *Schweiz. Arch. Tierheilk.* **105**, 337-345. Abstract 4090, *Veterinary Bulletin* 1963.

Cheeseman, C.L., & Mallinson, P.J. (1979). Radio tracking in the study of bovine tuberculosis in badgers. In *A Handbook on Biotelemetry and Radio Tracking:* 649-656. Almaner, C.J. & MacDonald, D.W. (Eds). Oxford, Pergamon Press.

Cheeseman, C.L. & Mallinson, P.J. (Submitted) Behaviour of Badgers *(meles meles)* infected with bovine tuberculosis. *Mammal Review.*

Coffey, D. (1977). Death to badgers? *New Scientist* **76** (1078), 430-431.

Cook, B.R. (1975). Tuberculosis in possums — Buller and Inangahua Counties. *Animal Health Division Special Report.* Ministry of Agriculture and Fisheries, Wellington, New Zealand.

Drabble, P. (1977). An assessment of gassing badgers. *The Field* **251** (6513), 994-995.

Drabble, P. (1978). No badgers in my wood. Michael Joseph.

Economic Advisory Council (1934). *Report by the Committee on Cattle Diseases.* Cmd 4591. HMSO, London.

Evans, H.T.J. & Thompson, H.V. (1980). Bovine tuberculosis in cattle in Great Britain, Part 1 — eradication of the disease from cattle and the role of the badger as a source of *Mycobacterium bovis* for cattle. *Animal Regulation Studies.* Elsevier, Amsterdam. In press.

Forest Research Institute (1975). Tuberculosis in opossums. *What's New in Forest Research.* Forest Research Institute, Private Bag, Rotorua, New Zealand.

Gallagher, J., Muirhead, R.H. & Burn. K.J. (1976). Tuberculosis in wild badgers in Gloucestershire: pathology. *Veterinary Record* **98**, 9-14.

Gallagher, J., Pill, A.H. & Muirhead, R.H. (1976). Badger translocations: a cruel kindness? (letter). *Veterinary Record* **98**, 205.

Gallagher, J. & Horwill, D. (1977). A selective oleic acid albumin agar medium for the cultivation of *Mycobacterium bovis. Journal of Hygiene, Cambridge* **79**, 155-160.

Gallagher, J. & Nelson, H. (1979). Cause of ill health and natural death in badgers in Gloucestershire. *Veterinary Record* **105**, 546-551.

Hellstrom, J. (1979). Success with TB possum purge. *Counterpest.*

Jones, D.M., Manton. V.J.A. & Cavanagh, P. (1976). Tuberculosis in a herd of Axis deer *(Axis axis)* at Whipsnade Park. *Veterinary Record* **98**, 525.

Jordan, L. (1933). The eradication of bovine tuberculosis. *Medical Research Council Special Report Series,* No. 184, HMSO, London.

Kruuk, H. (1978). Foraging and spatial organisation of the European badger *(Meles meles). Behavioural Ecology and Sociobiology* **4**, 75-89.

Kruuk, H. (1978). Spatial organisation and territorial behaviour of the European badger *(Meles meles). Journal of Zoology, London* **184**, 1-19.

Kruuk, H, & Parish, T. (1977). Behaviour of Badgers. *Institute of Terrestrial Ecology, Cambridge.*

Kruuk, H., Parish T., Brown, C.A.J., & Carrera, J. (1979). The use of pasture by the European badger *(Meles meles). Journal of Applied Ecology.* **16**, 453-459.

Little, T.W.A., Stuart, P. & Burn. K.J. (1975). Virulence for calves of tubercle bacillii isolated from badgers (letter). *Veterinary Record* **96**, 533.

Maurel, D. (1978). Seasonal changes of the testicular and thyroid functions in the badger *(Meles meles). Environmental Endocrinology.*

Maurel, D. & Boissin, J. (1979). Seasonal variations of thyroid activity in the adult male badger *(Meles meles). General and Comparative Endocrinology* **38**, 207-214.

McKeown, T. (1976). The modern rise of population. Edward Arnold.

Ministry of Agriculture, Fisheries and Food (1972). *Inquiry into bovine tuberculosis in West Cornwall.* London.

Ministry of Agriculture, Fisheries and Food (1977). *Badger control – code of practice.* HMSO. Bristol.

Ministry of Agriculture, Fisheries and Food (1979). *Bovine tuberculosis in badgers* — third report. London.

Ministry of Agriculture, Fisheries and Food (1979). *Badgers and bovine tuberculosis.* Tolworth Tower, Surbiton, Surrey.

Morris, J.A., Stevens, A.E., Stuart, P. & Little, T.W.A. (1979). A pilot study to assess the usefulness of ELISA in detecting tuberculosis in badgers. *Veterinary Record* **104**, 14.

Muirhead, R.H., Gallagher, J. & Burn. K.J. (1974). Tuberculosis in wild badgers in Gloucestershire: epidemiology. *Veterinary Record* **95**, 552-555.

Muirhead, R.H. & Gallagher, J. (1976). Badgers and bovine tuberculosis. *The Veterinary Annual,* 16th issue. John Wright, Bristol. 237-239.

Murray, R.R. (1970). Live trapping of badgers, their removal, release and rehabilitation in a new area. *Mammal Review* **1** (3), 86-92.

Murray, R.R. (1973). The requirements of badgers in captivity. In *The Welfare and Management of Wild Animals in Captivity.* University Federation for Animal Welfare, London.

Neal, E.G. (1977). *Badgers.* Blandford Press, Poole, Dorset.

New Zealand Ministry of Agriculture and Fisheries (1975). Possums as a source of tuberculosis infection for cattle. *Animal Health Division Special Report, Wellington.*

New Zealand Ministry of Agriculture and Fisheries (1975). TB in possums — Hohonu Mountain MAF/NZFS Project 117. *Animal Health Division Special Report, Wellington.*

R.S.P.C.A. (1979). Badgers and bovine tuberculosis: the case for further investigation. *Special Report.* Causeway, Horsham, West Sussex.

Scott, H.H. (1930). Tuberculosis in man and lower animals. *Medical Research Council Special Report Series, No. 149.* HMSO, London.

Printed in England for Her Majesty's Stationery Office by Robendene Ltd. Amersham.
Dd 696900 K18 9/80

no new ed 1/10
✓ NLS